Topics in Modern Poetry

Topics in Modern Poetry

Edited by *E. L. Black* MA MEd

Formerly Principal of
Middleton St George College of Education

John Murray

This anthology © E. L. Black 1982

First published 1982
by John Murray (Publishers) Ltd
50 Albemarle Street, London W1X 4BD

Printed in Great Britain by
Martin's Printing Works, Berwick-upon-Tweed

British Library Cataloguing in Publication Data
Topics in modern poetry.
  1..English poetry—20th century
  1. Black, E. L.
  821'.912'08   PR1225

ISBN 0-7195-3932-3

Preface

This anthology of poetry written since 1914, and especially since 1970, has been compiled with readers in the upper forms of schools and in colleges particularly in view. For this reason a number of good modern poems that are obscure, because they are densely packed with meaning or full of allusion, have been passed over in favour of other poems whose message is more easily grasped.

Is it possible, within these limitations, to give a characteristic selection of recent verse? I would argue that it is. In these pages will be found examples of many of the main trends in modern poetry. For instance, the tendency to express one's meaning with the utmost economy of words is visible enough here—but not in its more excessive forms. Similarly, the reader will quickly realize how readily present-day poets make use of the urgent and flexible rhythms of conversation, and how studiously most of them avoid stock 'poetic' phrases (such as 'Neptune's realm' for 'the sea'). Like Wordsworth, modern poets try to achieve intensity of feeling by using the language ordinary men and women employ in real life.

Not only in style but, I hope, in content also, this collection will give a fair, if necessarily sketchy, idea of what poets have been trying to do in recent decades. These poets write about many of the things that concerned their predecessors, but now with clearly discernible differences of emphasis.

As in earlier centuries, they write about birds and animals; but today they often focus on the freedom of the life of instinct in comparison with the regimentation that civilization imposes on human beings. They write, as many another poet did before them, of politics; but frequently in a way that makes it clear that the remedying of social evils is the central and consuming interest of their life. The beauty of town and countryside has long been a favourite topic of poets, but to many of the modern poets these are joys that are now threatened by human greed and folly. Above all, poets of this century, from Wilfred Owen and his contemporaries onwards, have written of war—no longer in the old heroic manner, but seeing it as an evil so great that perhaps only poetry can induce people to confront it sanely and squarely.

All these themes, and others, are to be found in this book. The division into sections provides an approximate indication of where a particular topic is treated; but poetry is really too rich and too diverse to be slotted neatly into categories, and many a poem will be found to spill over from one section into another.

January 1982   E. L. Black

Contents

PEOPLE WE MEET

MEMBERS OF THE FAMILY

Animals and Birds

THE RUNAWAY

Once when the snow of the year was beginning to fall,
We stopped by a mountain pasture to say, 'Whose colt?'
A little Morgan had one forefoot on the wall,
The other curled at his breast. He dipped his head
And snorted at us. And then he had to bolt.
We heard the miniature thunder where he fled,
And saw him, or thought we saw him, dim and grey,
Like a shadow against the curtain of falling flakes.
'I think the little fellow's afraid of the snow.
He isn't winter-broken. It isn't play
With the little fellow at all. He's running away.
I doubt if even his mother could tell him, "Sakes,
It's only weather." He'd think she didn't know!
Where is his mother? He can't be out alone.'
And now he comes again with clatter of stone,
And mounts the wall again with whited eyes
And all his tail that isn't hair up straight.
He shudders his coat as if to throw off flies.
'Whoever it is that leaves him out so late,
When other creatures have gone to stall and bin,
Ought to be told to come and take him in.'

Robert Frost

A MARCH CALF

Right from the start he is dressed in his best—his blacks and his
    whites.
Little Fauntleroy–quiffed and glossy,
A Sunday suit, a wedding natty get-up,
Standing in dunged straw

Under cobwebby beams, near the mud wall,
Half of him legs,
Shining-eyed, requiring nothing more
But that mother's milk come back often.

Everything else is in order, just as it is.
Let the summer skies hold off, for the moment.
This is just as he wants it.
A little at a time, of each new thing, is best.

Too much and too sudden is too frightening—
When I block the light, a bulk from space,
To let him in to his mother for a suck,
He bolts a yard or two, then freezes,

Staring from every hair in all directions,
Ready for the worst, shut up in his hopeful religion,
A little syllogism
With a wet blue-reddish muzzle, for God's thumb.

You see all his hopes bustling
As he reaches between the worn rails towards
The topheavy oven of his mother.
He trembles to grow, stretching his curl-tip tongue—

What did cattle ever find here
To make this dear little fellow
So eager to prepare himself?
He is already in the race, and quivering to win—

His new purpled eyeball swivel-jerks
In the elbowing push of his plans.
Hungry people are getting hungrier,
Butchers developing expertise and markets,

But he just wobbles his tail—and glistens
Within his dapper profile
Unaware of how his whole lineage
Has been tied up.

He shivers for feel of the world licking his side.
He is like an ember—one glow
Of lighting himself up
With the fuel of himself, breathing and brightening.

Soon he'll plunge out, to scatter his seething joy,
To be present at the grass,
To be free on the surface of such a wideness,
To find himself himself. To stand. To moo.

                                              Ted Hughes

AN OTTER

I

Underwater eyes, an eel's
Oil of water body, neither fish nor beast is the otter:
Four-legged yet water-gifted, to outfish fish;
With webbed feet and long ruddering tail
And a round head like an old tomcat.

Brings the legend of himself
From before wars or burials, in spite of hounds and vermin-poles;
Does not take root like the badger. Wanders, cries;
Gallops along land he no longer belongs to;
Re-enters the water by melting.

Of neither water nor land. Seeking
Some world lost when first he dived, that he cannot come at since,
Takes his changed body into the holes of lakes;
As if blind, cleaves the stream's push till he licks
The pebbles of the source; from sea

To sea crosses in three nights
Like a king in hiding. Crying to the old shape of the starlit land,
Over sunken farms where the bats go round,
Without answer. Till light and birdsong come
Walloping up roads with the milk wagon.

II

The hunt's lost him. Pads on mud,
Among sedges, nostrils a surface bead,
The otter remains, hours. The air,
Circling the globe, tainted and necessary,

Mingling tobacco-smoke, hounds and parsley,
Comes carefully to the sunk lungs.
So the self under the eye lies,
Attendant and withdrawn. The otter belongs

In double robbery and concealment—
From water that nourishes and drowns, and from land
That gave him his length and the mouth of the hound.
He keeps fat in the limpid integument

Reflections live on. The heart beats thick,
Big trout muscle out of the dead cold;
Blood is the belly of logic; he will lick
The fishbone bare. And can take stolen hold

On a bitch otter in a field full
Of nervous horses, but linger nowhere.
Yanked above hounds, reverts to nothing at all,
To this long pelt over the back of a chair.

Ted Hughes

THE CUNNING OF AN AGE

The fox sat under the hill.
And all around him the day was springing the earth
Curved away in a style he knew to be home;
The year grew around him like a love, the birds
Cried down the wind

And the air hummed with growing.
He smelt the humble plants at the foot of the hill.
The grass was bleeding like love and the insects stirred
In the air at ease with themselves. The black wind streamed
Over the top of the hill.

Only here had he made a home.
The ways of the world had stopped short of this bulge
On the surface of things because . . . because it had other
Things to do. And the fox sat under the hill
And all lay still.

Yet as he sat there wondering
How rivers came to be especially
His one at the edge of the world his world, a spot
Of red spat up at his eyes, no more, and was gone
In a twist of vision. No more than that

To the fox who sat under the hill.
The air was the same the year went round just the same
The insects turned around in their aimless journeys.
But just that red at the foot of the hill below
The stream had changed things.

Had changed his home
To a starting place, and below came the horn's winding
Warning halloo and up he was and smartly
Away as the red shot up to his horizon
And his mind's horizon.

And he was away.
No listening or waiting for the will and lust
Of the world but to live and lick his life
From the corners of a world that would hold him easily
Peacefully was his will,

Under a hill of maiden-hair
And grass as green as blood and summer-time
To sweat in his fur and his ways. He was off to save
His life. The hounds were baying the other side
Of the hill. And

He thought as he ran with his name
Of the names he'd been told and the games he'd been called, but the
    horn
Whirled round in his head and the hounds fell on
In the leaps that distance and time pulls on one, the tricks
The mind pulls on one.

And the wind changed his name
To FOLLOWED from FOX-ON-THE-HILL
And the wind followed, curling his brush. And the hounds followed
    too,
Like dreams like death on the hill like birds like grass
Like anything but not

Like fox he was
Or fox he knew and the horn curled round in his head
Slipping over the hill and into his head. But here
He swerved and hid. And the hounds went hurling past
With blood before

Their eyes, and the men and the world
With blood over their hands and a curse on their whips
And a horse on their world and a horn on their minds
Went for a day
　　Over and down the hill.

Jon Silkin

KANGAROO

In the northern hemisphere
Life seems to leap at the air, or skim under the wind
Like stags on rocky ground, or pawing horses, or springy scut-tailed
　　rabbits.

Or else rush horizontal to charge at the sky's horizon,
Like bulls or bisons or wild pigs.

Or slip like water slippery towards its ends,
As foxes, stoats, and wolves, and prairie dogs.

Only mice, and moles, and rats, and badgers, and beavers, and
　　perhaps bears
Seem belly-plumbed to the earth's mid-navel.
Or frogs that when they leap come flop, and flop to the centre of the
　　earth.

But the yellow antipodal Kangaroo, when she sits up,
Who can unseat her, like a liquid drop that is heavy, and just touches
　　earth?

The downward drip,
The down-urge.
So much denser than cold-blooded frogs.

Delicate mother Kangaroo
Sitting up there rabbit-wise, but huge, plump-weighted,
And lifting her beautiful slender face, oh, so much more gently and
　　finely lined than a rabbit's, or than a hare's,
Lifting her face to nibble at a round white peppermint drop which
　　she loves, sensitive mother Kangaroo.

Her sensitive, long, pure-bred face.
Her full antipodal eyes, so dark,
So big and quiet and remote, having watched so many empty dawns
   in silent Australia.

Her little loose hands, and drooping Victorian shoulders.
And then her great weight below the waist, her vast pale belly
With a thin young yellow little paw hanging out, and straggle of a
   long thin ear, like ribbon,
Like a funny trimming to the middle of her belly, thin little dangle of
   an immature paw, and one thin ear.

Her belly, her big haunches
And, in addition, the great muscular python-stretch of her tail.

There, she shan't have any more peppermint drops.
So she wistfully, sensitively sniffs the air, and then turns, goes off in
   slow sad leaps

On the long flat skis of her legs,
Steered and propelled by that steel-strong snake of a tail.

Stops again, half turns, inquisitive to look back.
While something stirs quickly in her belly, and a lean little face
   comes out, as from a window,
Peaked and a bit dismayed,
Only to disappear again quickly away from the sight of the world, to
   snuggle down in the warmth,
Leaving the trail of a different paw hanging out.

Still she watches with external, cocked wistfulness!
How full her eyes are, like the full, fathomless, shining eyes of
   an Australian black-boy
Who has been lost so many centuries on the margins of existence!
She watches with insatiable wistfulness.
Untold centuries of watching for something to come,
For a new signal from life, in that silent lost land of the South.

Where nothing bites but insects and snakes and the sun, small life,
Where no bull roared, no cow ever lowed, no stag cried, no leopard
   screeched, no lion coughed, no dog barked,
But all was silent save for parrots occasionally, in the haunted blue
   bush.

Wistfully watching, with wonderful liquid eyes.
And all her weight, all her blood, dripping sack-wise down towards
   the earth's centre,
And the live little-one taking in its paw at the door of her belly.

Leap then, and come down on the line that draws to the earth's
   deep, heavy centre.

D. H. Lawrence

LEOPARD

It was the night of the mess dance. Balloons on the bamboo walls,
The twirl of top brass, bags of off-duty bonhomie,
A spin of gin-bright wives whilst the scratched records hissed.
Outside was cooler. I found a night thick with crickets,
And a moon tangled in the thorn scrub.
There were fires glimmering on a far ridge
And, distantly, the drums of another dance.
By the thin track in front of me frogs
Grated the darkness. Everything pulsed.

A dog came out of the grass, head low and loping. Then
He stopped, one big foot
Lifted. Heavier than any
Dog. Tail flicking. I stood. Slowly
The head swung at me, and I saw eyes like lamps.
Behind me the music whined and the floor
Jogged. We watched each other, yards apart, waiting.
Then the eyes went out and he wasn't there.
The grass shivered after him.

Inside again, the lights, the noise, the walls,
The ordinariness held off the night's inhabitants,
Reducing again to rumour things
That prowled around out there.
Next morning, though, the pug marks
Scarred the smooth damp ground.

John Cassidy

THE JAGUAR

The apes yawn and adore their fleas in the sun.
The parrots shriek as if they were on fire, or strut
Like cheap tarts to attract the stroller with the nut.
Fatigued with indolence, tiger and lion

Lie still as the sun. The boa-constrictor's coil
Is a fossil. Cage after cage seems empty, or
Stinks of sleepers from the breathing straw.
It might be painted on a nursery wall.

But who runs like the rest past these arrives
At a cage where the crowd stands, stares, mesmerized,
As a child at a dream, at a jaguar hurrying enraged
Through prison darkness after the drills of his eyes

On a short fierce fuse. Not in boredom—
The eye satisfied to be blind in fire,
By the bang of blood in the brain deaf the ear—
He spins from the bars, but there's no cage to him

More than to the visionary his cell:
His stride is wildernesses of freedom:
The world rolls under the long thrust of his heel.
Over the cage floor the horizons come.

Ted Hughes

HYENA

I am waiting for you.
I have been travelling all morning through the bush
and not eaten.
I am lying at the edge of the bush
on a dusty path that leads from the burnt-out kraal.
I am panting, it is midday, I found no water-hole.
I am very fierce without food and although my eyes
are screwed to slits against the sun
you must believe I am prepared to spring.

What do you think of me?
I have a rough coat like Africa.
I am crafty with dark spots
like the bush-tufted plains of Africa.
I sprawl as a shaggy bundle of gathered energy
like Africa sprawling in its waters.
I trot, I lope, I slaver, I am a ranger.
I hunch my shoulders. I eat the dead.

Do you like my song?
When the moon pours hard and cold on the veldt
I sing, and I am the slave of darkness.
Over the stone walls and the mud walls and the ruined places
and the owls, the moonlight falls.
I sniff a broken drum. I bristle. My pelt is silver.
I howl my song to the moon—up it goes.
Would you meet me there in the waste places?

It is said I am a good match
for a dead lion. I put my muzzle
at his golden flanks, and tear. He
is my golden supper, but my tastes are easy.
I have a crowd of fangs, and I use them.
Oh and my tongue—do you like me
when it comes lolling out over my jaw
very long, and I am laughing?
I am not laughing.
But I am not snarling either, only
panting in the sun, showing you
what I grip
carrion with.

I am waiting
for the foot to slide,
for the heart to seize,
for the leaping sinews to go slack,
for the fight to the death to be fought to the death,
for a glazing eye and the rumour of blood.
I am crouching in my dry shadows
till you are ready for me.
My place is to pick you clean
and leave your bones to the wind.

Edwin Morgan

HAWK ROOSTING

I sit in the top of the wood, my eyes closed.
Inaction, no falsifying dream
Betweeen my hooked head and hooked feet:
Or in sleep rehearse perfect kills and eat.

The convenience of the high trees!
The air's buoyancy and the sun's ray
Are of advantage to me;
And the earth's face upward for my inspection.

My feet are locked upon the rough bark.
It took the whole of Creation
To produce my foot, my each feather:
Now I hold Creation in my foot

Or fly up, and revolve it all slowly—
I kill where I please because it is all mine.
There is no sophistry in my body:
My manners are tearing off heads—

The allotment of death.
For the one path of my flight is direct
Through the bones of the living.
No arguments assert my right:

The sun is behind me.
Nothing has changed since I began.
My eye has permitted no change.
I am going to keep things like this.

Ted Hughes

SOLITARY CROW

Why solitary crow? He in his feathers
Is a whole world of crow—of a dry-stick nest,
Of windy distances where to be crow is best,
Of tough-guy clowning and of black things done
To a sprawled lamb whose blood beads in the sun.

Sardonic anarchist. Where he goes he carried,
Since there's no centre, what a centre is,
And that is crow, the ragged self that's his.
Smudged on a cloud, he jeers at the world then halts
To jeer at himself and turns two somersaults.

He ambles through the air, flops down and seesaws
On a blunt fencepost, hiccups and says Caw.
The sun glints greasy on his working craw
And adds a silver spot to that round eye
Whose black light bends and cocks the world awry.

Norman MacCaig

BLUE-TITS

Bobbing among the fleecy willow-catkins
Acrobatic blue-tits swing and sway
In careful somersaults and neat gyrations,
Grub-picking deftly down each bending spray.

Blue and yellow, dusting yellow pollen,
One pecks a sparrow, drab among the gold,
Churrs and scolds in azure-crested anger
And scuttles down a twig all blue and bold
Defiance at this urchin gutter-haunter
Till all the blues combine against one grey
With active whirr and flutter, sound and thunder
On tiny wings to drive the foe away.

Blue-tit, white-cheeked like a painted toy
That jerks to life from some street-seller's string,
Twirls round twigs, his natural trapezes,
Darts to snap a moth upon the wing.
This plump-as-willow-catkin, primrose-breasted
And sky-capped morsel magnifies the Spring.

Phoebe Hesketh

THE STARLING

The starling is my darling, although
I don't much approve of its
Habits. Proletarian bird,
Nesting in holes and corners, making a mess,
And sometimes dropping its eggs
Just any old where—on the front lawn, for instance.

It thinks it can sing too. In springtime
They are on every rooftop, or high bough,
Or telegraph pole, blithering away
Discords, with clichés picked up
From the other melodists.

But go to Trafalgar Square,
And stand, about sundown, on the steps of St Martin's;
Mark then in the air
The starlings, before they roost, at their evolutions—
Scores of starlings, wheeling,
Streaming and twisting, the whole murmuration
Turning like one bird: an image
Realized, of the City.

John Heath-Stubbs

THE HERON

The cloud-backed heron will not move:
He stares into the stream.
He stands unfaltering while the gulls
And oyster-catchers scream.
He does not hear, he cannot see
The great white horses of the sea,
But fixes eyes on stillness
Below their flying team.

How long will he remain, how long
Have the grey woods been green?
The sky and the reflected sky,
Their glass he has not seen,
But silent as a speck of sand
Interpreting the sea and land,

13

His fall pulls down the fabric
Of all that windy scene.

Sailing with clouds and woods behind,
Pausing in leisured flight,
He stepped, alighting on a stone,
Dropped from the stars of night.
He stood there unconcerned with day,
Deaf to the tumult of the bay,
Watching a stone in water,
A fish's hidden light.

Sharp rocks drive back the breaking waves,
Confusing sea with air.
Bundles of spray blown mountain-high
Have left the shingle bare.
A shipwrecked anchor wedged by rocks,
Loosed by the thundering equinox,
Divides the herded waters,
The stallion and his mare.

Yet no distraction breaks the watch
Of that time-killing bird.
He stands unmoving on the stone;
Since dawn he has not stirred.
Calamity about him cries,
But he has fixed his golden eyes
On water's crooked tablet,
On light's reflected word.

Vernon Watkins

SWIFT

A peculiar dropout, a small fledgling swift,
Stayed with us for a while as a kind of guest.
Voracious, he sat on his belly all day
Squeaking as high as a bat, except when fed.

Streamlined for flight, yet too topheavy to fly
Or take to the air in which he was meant to live,
How might he leave the ground, though designed for the sky?
Happy to squeak and eat, he made no attempt.

14

Feet like talons, powerful to cling and grip,
The hooded greedy face of a predator,
He gobbled his meat like a dragon, remained fat,
Satisfied and demanding, until one day

The scimitar wings for no reason suddenly
Beat ten times to the second. He upended
Himself with furious flutters; keeled half over
Battering with black feathers at the level

Tabletop he'd been squatting on, and almost
Stood on his head. Nothing would keep him quiet.
Having made clear to us that his time had come
He was ready to go, our pensioner of a fortnight.

We fetched him out to a field, carried in the palm
Of a hand; bowled the soft body like a ball
Into the air, which received him falling, but
His wings found their element, then scissoring

With panic sleight, bore the surprised and able
Creature to his inheritance; who sank,
Lifted and sank, with fear and confidence
Exulting into the distance, out of our sight.

David Wright

OWL

is my favourite. Who flies
like a nothing through the night,
who-whoing. Is a feather
duster in leafy corners ring-a-rosy-ing
boles of mice. Twice

you hear him call. Who
is he looking for? You hear
him hoovering over the floor
of the wood. O would you be gold
rings in the driving skull

15

if you could? Hooded and
vulnerable by the winter suns
owl looks. Is the grain or bark
in the dark. Round beaks are at
work in the pellety nest,

resting. Owl is an eye
in the barn. For a hole
in the trunk owl's blood
is to blame. Black talons in the
petrified fur! Cold walnut hands

on the case of the brain! In the reign
of the chicken owl comes like
a god. Is a goad in
the rain to the pink eyes,
dripping. For a meal in the day

flew, killed, on the moor. Six
mouths are the seed of his
arc in the season. Torn meat
from the sky. Owl lives
by the claws of his brain. On the branch

in the sever of the hand's
twigs owl is a backward look.
Flown wind in the skin. Fine
rain in the bones. Owl breaks
like the day. Am an owl, am an owl.

George MacBeth

Political and Social Problems

PROGRESS

When the armies marched off,
Cursing the criminal stupidity of their leaders,
To fight for the glory and prosperity
Of the motherland,
The leaders
Did their bit

By putting the prices up;
And when the remnants came back,
Cursing the criminal stupidity of their leaders,
Their leaders did what they could for them
By putting the prices up again.
This so reduced
The prosperity of the country
That new leaders were appointed
Whose criminal stupidity was no less
Than the first.

The only consoling thought is
That somewhere along the line
The idea of glory
Was lost sight of.

Norman MacCaig

HOMAGE TO A GOVERNMENT

Next year we are to bring the soldiers home
For lack of money, and it is all right.
Places they guarded, or kept orderly,
Must guard themselves, and keep themselves orderly.

We want the money for ourselves at home
Instead of working. And this is all right.

It's hard to say who wanted it to happen,
But now it's been decided nobody minds.
The places are a long way off, not here,
Which is all right, and from what we hear
The soldiers there only made trouble happen.
Next year we shall be easier in our minds.

Next year we shall be living in a country
That brought its soldiers home for lack of money.
The statues will be standing in the same
Tree-muffled squares, and look nearly the same.
Our children will not know it's a different country.
All we can hope to leave them now is money.

Philip Larkin

THE PERSIAN VERSION

Truth-loving Persians do not dwell upon
The trivial skirmish fought near Marathon.
As for the Greek theatrical tradition
Which represents that summer's expedition
Not as a mere reconnaissance in force
By three brigades of foot and one of horse
(Their left flank covered by some obsolete
Light craft detached from the main Persian fleet)
But as a grandiose, ill-starred attempt
To conquer Greece—they treat it with contempt;
And only incidentally refute
Major Greek claims, by stressing what repute
The Persian monarch and the Persian nation
Won by this salutary demonstration:
Despite a strong defence and adverse weather
All arms combined magnificently together.

Robert Graves

News Editor: Peer Confesses,
Bishop Undresses,
Torso Wrapped in Rug,
Girl Guide Throttled,
Baronet Bottled,
J.P. Goes to Jug.

But yesterday's story's
Old and hoary.
Never mind who got hurt.
No use grieving,
Let's get weaving.
What's the latest dirt?

Diplomat Spotted,
Scout Garrotted,
Thigh Discovered in Bog,
Wrecks Off Barmouth,
Sex in Yarmouth
Woman In Love With Dog,
Eminent Hostess Shoots Her Guests,
Harrogate Lovebird Builds Two Nests.

Cameraman: *Builds two nests?*
Shall I get a picture of the lovebird singing?
Shall I get a picture of her pretty little eggs?
Shall I get a picture of her babies?

News Editor: No!
Go and get a picture of her legs.

Beast Slays Beauty,
Priest Flays Cutie,
Cupboard Shows Tell-Tale Stain,
Mate Drugs Purser,
Dean Hugs Bursar,
Mayor Binds Wife with Chain,
Elderly Monkey Marries For Money,
Jilted Junky Says 'I Want My Honey'.

Cameraman: *'Want my honey?'*
Shall I get a picture of the pollen flying?

19

Shall I get a picture of the golden dust?
Shall I get a picture of a queen bee?

News Editor: No!
        Go and get a picture of her bust.

        Judge Gets Frisky,
        Nun Drinks Whisky,
        Baby Found Burnt in Cot,
        Show Girl Beaten,
        Duke Leaves Eton—

Cameraman: Newspaper Man Gets Shot!
              May all things clean
              And fresh and green
              Have mercy upon your soul,
              Consider yourself paid
              By the hole my bullet made—

News Editor   (*dying*): Come and get a picture of the hole.

Paul Dehn

ATTACK ON THE AD-MAN

This trumpeter of nothingness, employed
To keep our reason dull and null and void,
This man of wind and froth and flux will sell
The wares of any who reward him well.
Praising whatever he is paid to praise,
He hunts for ever-newer, smarter ways
To make the gilt seem gold; the shoddy, silk;
To cheat us legally; to bluff and bilk
By methods which no jury can prevent
Because the law's not broken, only bent.

This mind for hire, this mental prostitute
Can tell the half-lie hardest to refute;
Knows how to hide an inconvenient fact
And when to leave a doubtful claim unbacked;
Manipulates the truth but not too much,
And, if his patter needs the Human Touch,
Skilfully artless, artfully naive,
Wears his convenient heart upon his sleeve.

He uses words that once were strong and fine,
Primal as sun and moon and bread and wine,
True, honourable, honoured, clear and clean,
And leaves them shabby, worn, diminished, mean.
He takes ideas and trains them to engage
In the long little wars big combines wage.
He keeps his logic loose, his feelings flimsy;
Turns eloquence to cant and wit to whimsy;
Trims language till it fits his client's pattern
And style's a glossy tart or limping slattern.

He studies our defences, finds the cracks
And, where the wall is weak or worn, attacks.
He finds the fear that's deep, the wound that's tender,
And, mastered, outmanoeuvred, we surrender.
We who have tried to choose accept his choice
And tired succumb to his untiring voice.
The dripping tap makes even granite soften.
We trust the brand-name we have heard so often
And join the queue of sheep that flock to buy;
We fools who know our folly, you and I.

A. S. J. Tessimond

TO OUR CATCHMENT BOARD

Startling all spirits, dreams, and secrets
Out of the woods that verged on my first river,
The engineers arrived, large friendly men
With much tobacco armed, and drainage schemes.
They had no special hate against my river,
And indeed loved it, as a henwife loves
Some fated fowl, 'Regardez, qu'elle est belle'.
With truck and shovel, chain and claw, horse-power
Obeyed the office; hawthorns thought immortal
Found they were not, and oaks of kingliest antler
Left their old vantage over my first river.
Needs not to tell that flag and sedge and plantain
From humbler camp, but privileged, were sacked,
And snags that poked their snouts above the stream
In summer, trying to be crocodiles,
Were soon exposed ashore for what they were.
In mathematic channels reinforced

With best cement (as far as means would run)
The river took his solitary way.
Catchment as catchment can, and I'll not say
The work was wrong.
                              For I have known my river
Since this brave century opened, and have noted
A certain permanence, a personality,
A liking almost for each opposition,
A willingness to make the best of things.
And now the foreman and his squad and tackle
Have moved a few miles on, and the wilful stream
Invents new rippling-places and underminings,
Long strands and sands; by whose example moved
The willow-wood may gather, the full moon
Sow sacred oaks, and some new child in time
Find in their shadow forms of grace I found,
And by their dance and by the wavelets' chime
Be blest till sense in deeper floods be drowned.

Edmund Blunden

A SMALL WAR

Climbing from Merthyr through the dew of August mornings
When I was a centaur-cyclist, on the skills of wheels
I'd loop past the Storey Arms, past streaming lorries
Stopped for flasks of early tea, and fall into Breconshire.
A thin road under black Fan Frynych—which keeps its winter
Shillings long through Spring—took me to the Senni valley.

That was my plenty, to rest on the narrow saddle
Looking down on the farms, letting the simple noises
Come singly up. It was there I saw a ring-ousel
Wearing the white gash of his mountains; but every
Sparrow's feather in that valley was rare, golden,
Perfect. It was an Eden fourteen miles from home.

Evan Drew, my second cousin, lived there, a long, slow man
With a brown gaze I remember him. From a hill farm
Somewhere on the slopes above Heol Senni he sent his sons,
Boys a little older than I, to the Second World War.
They rode their ponies to the station, they waved
Goodbye, they circled the spitting sky above Europe.

I would not fight for Wales, the great battle-cries
Do not arouse me. I keep short boundaries holy,
Those my eyes have recognised and my heart has known
As welcome. Nor would I fight for her language. I spend
My few pence of Welsh to amuse my friends, to comment
On the weather. They carry no thought that could be mine.

It's the small wars I understand. So now that forty
People lock their gates in Senni, keeping the water out
With frailest barrier of love and anger, I'd fight for them.
Five miles of land, enough small farms to make a heaven,
Are easily trapped on the drawing-board, a decision
Of the pen drowns all. Yes, the great towns need

The humming water, yes, I have taken my rods to other
Swimming valleys and happily fished above the vanished
Fields. I know the arguments. It is a handful of earth
I will not argue with, and the slow cattle swinging weightily
Home. When I open the taps in my English bathroom
I am surprised they do not run with Breconshire blood.

Leslie Norris

JONES THE GROCER

Jones the Grocer, we called him—
A pale man, skilled in servility,
His hands white and soft as the lard he stacked
In small, meticulous rows, his head
Polished and somehow apologetic, as if
He was crowned forever with dishonour.

I hated him, he was too obsequious by far,
Embellishing transactions with fulsome flattery
Of your habits, your appearance, your miserable opinions.
He seemed to exist in a fog
Of self-effacement, through which one caught
The rarest glimpse of a human dignity.

Yet one could suffer the arid washing of his hands
For the joy of that shop, its curiosities,
Like the corner where it was always dusk
And equatorial, aromatic with coffee beans;

And the calendars derisive of topicality,
And the adverts twenty years out of date.

One could suffer it, and gladly suffer it again
To be delivered of this, its successor—
A supermarket, slick and soulless,
Arrogantly accepting the shoppers' homage.

Herbert Williams

TELEPHONE CONVERSATION

The price seemed reasonable, location
Indifferent. The landlady swore she lived
Off premises. Nothing remained
But self-confession. 'Madam', I warned,
'I hate a wasted journey—I am African.'
Silence. Silenced transmission of
Pressurized good-breeding. Voice, when it came,
Lipstick coated, long gold-rolled
Cigarette-holder pipped. Caught I was, foully.
'HOW DARK?' . . . I had not misheard . . . 'ARE YOU LIGHT
OR VERY DARK?' Button B. Button A. Stench
Of rancid breath of public hide-and-speak.
Red booth. Red pillar-box. Red double-tiered
Omnibus squelching tar. It *was* real! Shamed
By ill-mannered silence, surrender
Pushed dumbfounded to beg simplification.
Considerate she was, varying the emphasis—
'ARE YOU DARK? OR VERY LIGHT?' Revelation came.
'You mean—like plain or milk chocolate?'
Her assent was clinical, crushing in its light
Impersonality. Rapidly, wave-length adjusted,
I chose. 'West African sepia'—and as afterthought
'Down in my passport.' Silence for spectroscopic
Flight of fancy, till truthfulness clanged her accent
Hard on the mouthpiece. 'WHAT'S THAT?' conceding
'DON'T KNOW WHAT THAT IS.' 'Like brunette.'
'THAT'S DARK, ISN'T IT?' 'Not altogether.
Facially, I am brunette, but madam, you should see
The rest of me. Palm of my hand, soles of my feet
Are a peroxide blonde. Friction, caused—
Foolishly madam—by sitting down, has turned

My bottom raven black—One moment madam!'—sensing
Her receiver rearing on the thunderclap
About my ears—'Madam,' I pleaded, 'wouldn't you rather
See for yourself?'

Wole Soyinka

THIS LANDSCAPE, THESE PEOPLE

I

My eighth spring in England I walk among
   The silver birches of Putney Heath,
   Stepping over twigs and stones: being stranger,
   I see but do not touch: only the earth
   Permits an attachment. I do not wish
To be seen, and move, eyes at my sides, like a fish.

And do they notice me, I wonder, these
   Englishmen strolling with stiff country strides?
   I lean against a tree, my eyes are knots
   In its bark, my skin the wrinkles in its sides.
   I leap hedges, duck under chestnut boughs,
And through the black clay let my swift heels trail like ploughs.

A child at a museum, England for me
   Is an exhibit within a glass case.
   The country, like an antique chair, has a rope
   Across it. I may not sit, only pace
   Its frontiers. I slip through ponds, jump ditches,
Through galleries of ferns see England in pictures.

II

My seventeen years in India, I swam
   Along the silver beaches of Bombay,
   Pulled coconuts from the sky and tramped
   Red horizons with the swagger and sway
   Of Romantic youth; with the impudence
Of a native tongue, I cried for independence.

A troupe came to town, marched through villages;
  Began with two tight-rope walkers, eyes gay
  And bamboos and rope on their bare shoulders;
  A snake-charmer joined them, beard long and grey,
  Baskets of cobras on his turbaned head;
Through villages marched: children, beating on drums, led

Them from village to village, and jugglers
  Joined them and swallowers of swords, eaters
  Of fire brandishing flames through the thick air,
  Jesters with tongues obscene as crows', creatures
  Of the earth: stray dogs, lean jackals, a cow;
Stamping, shouting, entertaining, making a row

From village to village they marched to town;
  Conjurors to bake bread out of earth, poets
  To recite epics at night. The troupe, grown
  Into a nation, halted, squirmed: the sets
  For its act, though improvised, were re-cast
From the frames of an antique, slow-moving, dead past.

India halted: as suddenly as a dog,
  Barking, hangs out his tongue, stifles his cry.
  An epic turned into a monologue
  Of death. The rope lay stiff across the country;
  All fires were eaten, swallowed all the swords;
The horizons paled, then thickened, blackened with crows.

Born to this continent, all was mine
  To pluck and taste: pomegranates to purple
  My tongue and chillies to burn my mouth. Stones
  Were there to kick. This landscape, these people—
  Bound by the rope and consumed by their own fire.
Born here, among these people, I was a stranger.

III

This landscape, these people! Silver birches
  With polished trunks chalked around a chestnut.
  All is fall-of-night still. No thrush reaches
  Into the earth for worms, nor pulls at the root
  Of a crocus. Dogs have led their masters home.
I stroll, head bowed, hearing only the sound of loam

At my heel's touch. Now I am intimate
  With England; we meet, secret as lovers.
  I pluck leaves and speak into the air's mouth;
  As a woman's hair, I deck with flowers
  The willow's branches; I sit by the pond,
My eyes are stars in its stillness; as with a wand,

I stir the water with a finger until
  It tosses waves, until countries appear
  From its dark bed: the road from Putney Hill
  Runs across oceans into the harbour
  Of Bombay. To this country I have come.
Stranger or an inhabitant, this is my home.

Zulfikar Ghose

RACE

  When I returned to my home town
  believing that no one would care
  who I was and what I thought
  it was as if the people caught
  an echo of me everywhere
  they knew my story by my face
  and I who am always alone
  became a symbol of my race

  Like every living Jew I have
  in imagination seen
  the gas-chamber the mass-grave
  the unknown body which was mine
  and found in every German face
  behind the mask the mark of Cain
  I will not make their thoughts my own
  by hating people for their race

Karen Gershon

THE ROMANIES IN TOWN

let us leave this place, brother,
it is not for us
they have built a great city
with broken glass
see how it shimmers in the evening light?

their feet are bleeding
through walking on splinters
they pretend not to notice

they have offered us a house
with cabbages in the garden
they tell us of their strange country
and want us to stay
and help them fight for it

do not listen, brother,
they will bind you with promises
and with hope
on all sides stretch fields of rubble
they say we should admire the view

the young are busy building
new glass palaces
they gather up the splinters
and bathe their feet with tears

come quick come quick
we will take the road towards the sea
we will pick blackberries
from hedges in the lanes
we will pitch camp on empty moors
and watch the hawk skimming
above the trees

but if we do not fight
the hawks will die, sister,
they have no time for wild birds
and will shoot us down.

Anne Beresford

GEOGRAPHY LESSON

When the jet sprang into the sky,
it was clear why the city
had developed the way it had,
seeing it scaled six inches to the mile.
There seemed an inevitability
about what on ground had looked haphazard,
unplanned and without style
when the jet sprang into the sky.

When the jet reached ten thousand feet,
it was clear why the country
had cities where rivers ran
and why the valleys were populated.
The logic of geography—
that land and water attracted man—
was clearly delineated
when the jet reached ten thousand feet.

When the jet rose six miles high,
it was clear that the earth was round
and that it had more sea than land.
But it was difficult to understand
that the men on the earth found
causes to hate each other, to build
walls across cities and to kill.
From that height, it was not clear why.

Zulfikar Ghose

THE EXPLOSION

On the day of the explosion
Shadows pointed towards the pithead:
In the sun the slagheap slept.

Down the lane came men in pitboots
Coughing oath-edged talk and pipe-smoke,
Shouldering off the freshened silence.

One chased after rabbits; lost them;
Came back with a nest of lark's eggs;
Showed them; lodged them in the grasses.

So they passed in beards and moleskins,
Fathers, brothers, nicknames, laughter,
Through the tall gates standing open.

At noon, there came a tremor; cows
Stopped chewing for a second; sun,
Scarfed as in a heat-haze, dimmed.

The dead go on before us, they
Are sitting in God's house in comfort,
We shall see them face to face—

Plain as lettering in the chapels
It was said, and for a second
Wives saw men of the explosion

Clearer than in life they managed—
Gold as on a coin, or walking
Somehow from the sun towards them,

One showing the eggs unbroken.

Philip Larkin

THE HOUSES

Forlorn and glum the couples go
While Capital and Labour fight.
For lack of homes they can't unite
And love says 'Yes,' the builders, 'No.'

Yet, troubling not for time nor rest,
The courting rooks be flying thick,
And not a beak wi'out a stick
And not an elm wi'out a nest.

It do cast down my ancient mind
How senseless fowls can run their show,
Marry and help their childer grow,
And not us clever human kind.

Lords of creation we may be,
Though what the mischief we creates
But trouble, taxes, higher rates,
Be damned to us if I can see.

Eden Philpotts

from SCHOOL'S OUT

Whatever did we learn at Summerhill?
No maths, no hangups; how to play *Dear Brutus*.
It wasn't doing barbola on the mantelpiece
with red-hot pokers, breaking windows all day
or maidenheads all night—though you'd think so
to hear the critics. And did Neill set us free?
You never know with voluntary lessons,
they crouch there in your path like friendly enemies,
you pat them or you sidle past, knowing
you can't play truant when you're free already.
School government was on our hunkers, noisy,
fizzing, seesawing, Neill won, we won, no one won
while the long shadows gathered on the chintz.
We were Hitler's autobahns in reverse,
anti-Stakhanovites, our trains would never
run on time. 'If I create a millionaire'
cried Neill 'I've failed!' But capitalism
slid on its way despite our lost repressions.
We tinkered in the workshop, made toy guns
but never robbed a bank or even knew
half Europe had been robbed. Now if you ask
what I think of it I honestly don't know,
    it was great but I .
    honestly don't know.

Ivan Illich bought a big new broom.
'Most people learn most things out of school.'
Why not junk the institution then?
The point was we had reached the stage we could.
Access! access! was his cry, and timetables, textbooks,
exams, walls, bells were as much garbage
as last year's Cadillac. Plug in! playback!
tapespond! The electronic network longs
to set you free. The what and where and when

of learning's in your own hands now. Deschool.
Decamp. Disperse. The player and the game
are one, nobody prods men to the board.
—So we were the first tape and data children,
we've been through the tube, come out, still cool.
We know how Armstrong landed, bleeps call us
in our breast-pockets everywhere we go,
we've got cassettes of Basque folk-songs, slides
of the water-flea, microfilm drips from us
in clusters, if there's music of the spheres
we've heard it. I've been talking to the dolphins
in California, and they say they've seen
a school (which I know is impossible)
   far out in the bay.
   Whales, whales, you fool.

Edwin Morgan

INEXPENSIVE PROGRESS

Encase your legs in nylons,
Bestride your hills with pylons
   O age without a soul;
Away with gentle willows
And all the elmy billows
   That through your valleys roll.

Let's say good-bye to hedges
And roads with grassy edges
   And winding country lanes;
Let all things travel faster
Where motor-car is master
   Till only Speed remains.

Destroy the ancient inn-signs
But strew the roads with tin signs
   'Keep Left', 'M4', 'Keep Out!'
Command, instruction, warning,
Repetitive adorning
   The rockeried roundabout;

For every raw obscenity
Must have its small 'amenity',
    Its patch of shaven green,
And hoardings look a wonder
In banks of floribunda
    With floodlights in between.

Leave no old village standing
Which could provide a landing
    For aeroplanes to roar,
But spare such cheap defacements
As huts with shattered casements
    Unlived-in since the war.

Let no provincial High Street
Which might be your or my street
    Look as it used to do.
But let the chain stores place here
Their miles of black glass facia
    And traffic thunder through.

And if there is some scenery,
Some unpretentious greenery,
    Surviving anywhere,
It does not need protecting
For soon we'll be erecting
    A power station there.

When all our roads are lighted
By concrete monsters sited
    Like gallows overhead,
Bathed in the yellow vomit
Each monster belches from it,
    We'll know that we are dead.

John Betjeman

A CURSE

Dark was that day when Diesel
conceived his grim engine that
begot you, vile invention,

more vicious, more criminal
than the camera even,
metallic monstrosity,
bale and bane of our Culture,
chief woe of our Commonweal.

How dare the Law prohibit
hashish and heroin yet
license your use, who inflate
all weak inferior egos?
Their addicts only do harm
to their own lives: you poison
the lungs of the innocent,
your din dithers the peaceful,
and on choked roads hundreds must
daily die by chance-medley.

Nimble technicians, surely
you should hang your heads in shame.
Your wit works mighty wonders,
has landed men on the Moon,
replaced brains by computers,
and can smith a 'smart' bomb.
It is a crying scandal
that you cannot take the time
or be bothered to build us,
what sanity knows we need,
an odourless and noiseless
staid little electric brougham.

W. H. Auden

TRANSLATION

Now that the barbarians have got as far as Picra,
And all the new music is written in the twelve tone scale,
And I am anyway approaching my fortieth birthday,
    I will dissemble no longer.

I will stop expressing my belief in the rosy
Future of man, and accept the evidence
Of a couple of wretched wars and innumerable
    Abortive revolutions.

I will cease to blame the stupidity of the slaves
Upon their masters and nurture, and will say,
Plainly, that they are enemies to culture,
    Advancement and cleanliness.

From progressive organisations, from quarterlies
Devoted to daring verse, from membership of
Committees, from letters of various protest
    I shall withdraw forthwith.

When they call me reactionary I shall smile
Secure in another dimension. When they say
'Cinna has ceased to matter' I shall know
    How well I reflect the times.

The ruling class will think I am on their side
And make friendly overtures, but I shall retire
To the side furthest from Picra and write some poems
    About the doom of the whole boiling.

Anyone happy in this age and place
Is daft or corrupt. Better to abdicate
From a material and spiritual terrain
    Fit only for barbarians.

Roy Fuller

People We Meet

PUBLIC-HOUSE CONFIDENCE

Well, since you're from the other side of town,
I'll tell you how I hold a soft job down.
In the designing-rooms and laboratory
I'm dressed in overalls, and so pretend
To be on business from the factory.
The workmen think I'm from the other end.
The in-betweens and smart commission-men
Believe I must have some pull with the boss.
So, playing off the spanner against the pen,
I never let the rumour get across
Of how I am no use at all to either,
And draw the pay of both for doing neither.

Norman Cameron

EXECUTIVE

I am a young executive. No cuffs than mine are cleaner;
I have a Slimline brief-case and I use the firm's Cortina.
In every roadside hostelry from here to Burgess Hill
The *maitres d'hôtel* all know me well and let me sign the bill.

You ask me what it is I do. Well actually, you know,
I'm partly a liaison man and partly P.R.O.
Essentially I integrate the current export drive
And basically I'm viable from ten o'clock till five.

For vital off-the-record work – that's talking transport-wise –
I've a scarlet Aston-Martin – and does she go? She flies!
Pedestrians and dogs and cats – we mark them down for slaughter.
I also own a speed-boat which has never touched the water.

She's built of fibre-glass, of course. I call her 'Mandy Jane'
After a bird I used to know – No soda, please, just plain –
And how did I acquire her? Well to tell you about that
And to put you in the picture I must wear my other hat.

I do some mild developing. The sort of place I need
Is a quiet country market town that's rather run to seed.
A luncheon and a drink or two, a little *savoir faire* –
I fix the Planning Officer, the Town Clerk and the Mayor.

And if some preservationist attempts to interfere
A 'dangerous structure' notice from the Borough Engineer
Will settle any buildings that are standing in our way –
The modern style, sir, with respect, has really come to stay.

John Betjeman

THE YOUNG ONES

They slip on to the bus, hair piled up high.
New styles each month, it seems to me. I look,
Not wanting to be seen, casting my eye
Above the unread pages of a book.

They are fifteen or so. When I was thus,
I huddled in school coats, my satchel hung
Lop-sided on my shoulder. Without fuss
These enter adolescence; being young

Seems good to them, a state we cannot reach,
No talk of 'awkward ages' now. I see
How childish gazes staring out of each
Unfinished face prove me incredibly

Old-fashioned. Yet at least I have the chance
To size up several stages—young yet old,
Doing the twist, mocking an 'old-time' dance:
So many ways to be unsure or bold.

Elizabeth Jennings

THE CLOTHES PIT

The young women are obsessed with beauty.
Their old-fashioned sewing machines rattle in Terry Street.
They must keep up, they must keep up.

They wear teasing skirts and latest shoes,
Lush, impermanent coats, American cosmetics.
But they lack intellectual grooming.

In the culture of clothes and little philosophies,
They only have clothes. They do not need to be seen
Carrying a copy of *International Times*,

Or the *Liverpool Poets*, the wish to justify their looks
With things beyond themselves. They mix up colours,
And somehow they are often fat and unlovely.

They don't get high on pot, but get sick on cheap
Spanish Burgundy, or beer in rampant pubs,
And come home supported and kissed and bad-tempered.

But they have clothes, bright enough to show they dream
Of places other than this, an inarticulate paradise,
Eating exotic fowl in sunshine with courteous boys.

Three girls go down the street with the summer wind.
The litter of pop rhetoric blows down Terry Street,
Bounces past their feet, into their lives.

Douglas Dunn

BLACK JACKETS

In the silence that prolongs the span
Rawly of music when the record ends,
The red-haired boy who drove a van
In weekday overalls but, like his friends,

Wore cycle boots and jacket here
To suit the Sunday hangout he was in,
Heard, as he stretched back from his beer,
Leather creak softly round his neck and chin.

Before him, on a coal-black sleeve
Remote exertion had lined, scratched, and burned
Insignia that could not revive
The heroic fall or climb where they were earned.

On the other drinkers bent together,
Concocting selves for their impervious kit,
He saw it as no more than leather
Which, taut across the shoulders grown to it,

Sent through the dimness of a bar
As sudden and anonymous hints of light
As those that shipping give, that are
Now flickers in the Bay, now lost in night.

He stretched out like a cat, and rolled
The bitterish taste of beer upon his tongue,
And listened to a joke being told:
The present was the things he stayed among.

If it was only loss he wore,
He wore it to assert, with fierce devotion,
Complicity and nothing more.
He recollected his initiation,

And one especially of the rites.
For on his shoulders they had put tattoos:
The group's name on the left, The Knights,
And on the right the slogan *Born To Lose*.

Thom Gunn

ON THE MOVE

'Man, you gotta Go'

The blue jay scuffling in the bushes follows
Some hidden purpose, and the gust of birds
That spurts across the field, the wheeling swallows,
Have nested in the trees and undergrowth.
Seeking their instinct, or their poise, or both,
One moves with an uncertain violence
Under the dust thrown by a baffled sense
Or the dull thunder of approximate words.

On motorcycles, up the road, they come:
Small, black, as flies hanging in heat, the Boys,
Until the distance throws them forth, their hum
Bulges to thunder held by calf and thigh.
In goggles, donned impersonality,
In gleaming jackets trophied with the dust,
They strap in doubt—by hiding it, robust—
And almost hear a meaning in their noise.

Exact conclusion of their hardiness
Has no shape yet, but from known whereabouts
They ride, direction where the tyres press.
They scare a flight of birds across the field:
Much that is natural, to the will must yield.
Men manufacture both machine and soul,
And use what they imperfectly control
To dare a future from the taken routes.

It is part solution, after all.
One is not necessarily discord
On earth; or damned because, half animal,
One lacks direct instinct, because one wakes
Afloat on movement that divides and breaks.
One joins the movement in a valueless world,
Choosing it, till, both hurler and the hurled,
One moves as well, always toward, toward.

A minute holds them, who have come to go:
The self-defined, astride the created will
They burst away; the towns they travel through
Are home for neither bird nor holiness,
For birds and saints complete their purposes.
At worst, one is in motion; and at best,
Reaching no absolute, in which to rest,
One is always nearer by not keeping still.

Thom Gunn

PROVINCIAL UNDERGRADUATE

The draggled hair, stained sweater, rumpled slacks,
Eyes staring angrily out of a young face,
Hand nervously dabbing a cigarette

Out against a wall as though it was somebody's face.
He grunts, not argues, grins rather than laughs when
Somebody's tried to do something and failed again.

That somebody! How he hates him! Whoever he is—
From a better school, maybe, or dressed up to kill,
Who can grow a beard, throw parties, pay out cash,
Who can always get the prettiest girls at will.
He covertly kicks his ankles in a queue,
Or lounges across his path. What else can he do?

'After puberty, only the glands want to learn'
Says Goole who weighs up students at a sneer
And finds them wanting. Wanting to get out and earn,
Wanting to be loved, respected,—maybe, feared.
A place in the world? A good job? Goole, you
Failed to teach him what else there was to do.

What else *is* there? He's got to get a degree
Somehow, writes essays on half-known facts.
They're ticked, gone over, somehow rejected. He
Must do better next time, re-read, re-think, go back—
Go back in anger, resign, though not resigned,
Looking for what he does not want to find.

Philip Hobsbaum

OFFICE PARTY

We were throwing out small-talk
On the smoke-weary air,
When the girl with the squeaker
Came passing each chair.

She was wearing a white dress,
Her paper-hat was a blue
Crown with a red tassel,
And to every man who

Glanced up at her, she leant over
And blew down the hole,
So the squeaker inflated
And began to unroll.

41

She stopped them all talking
With this trickery,
And she didn't leave out anyone
Until she came to me.

I looked up and she met me
With a half-teasing eye
And she took a mild breath and
Went carefully by,

And with cold concentration
To the next man she went,
And squawked out the instrument
To its fullest extent.

And whether she passed me
Thinking that it would show
Too much favour to mock me
I never did know—

Or whether her withholding
Was her cruelty,
And it was that she despised me,
I couldn't quite see—

So it could have been discretion,
And it could have been disgust,
But it was quite unequivocal,
And suffer it I must:

All I know was: she passed me,
Which I did not expect
—And I'd never so craved for
Some crude disrespect.

Alan Brownjohn

A MYSTERY AT EUSTON

The train is still, releasing one loud sigh.
Doors swing and slam, porters importune.
The pigskin labelled luggage of the rich
Is piled on trolleys, rolled to waiting cars,

Grey citizens lug baggage to the place
Where fluttering kisses, craning welcomes wait.
A hoarse voice speaks from heaven, but not to her,
The girl whose luggage is a tartan grip
With broken zip, white face a tiny kite
Carried on the currents of the crowd.
The handsome stranger did not take her bag,
No talent-scout will ask her out to dine.
Her tights are laddered and her new shoes wince.
The Wimpy bar awaits, the single room,
The job as waitress, golden-knuckled ponce.
Whatever place she left—Glasgow, Leeds,
The village on the moors—there's no return.
Beyond the shelter of the station, rain
Veils the day and wavers at a gust,
Then settles to its absent-minded work
As if it has forgotten how to rest.

Vernon Scannell

GOOD FRIDAY

Three o'clock. The bus lurches
round into the sun. 'D's this go—'
he flops beside me—'right along Bath Street?
—Oh tha's, tha's all right, see I've
got to get some Easter eggs for the kiddies.
I've had a wee drink, ye understand—
ye'll maybe think it's a—funny day
to be celebrating—well, no, but ye see
I wasny working, and I like to celebrate
when I'm no working—I don't say it's right
I'm no saying it's right, ye understand—ye understand?
But anyway tha's the way I look at it—
I'm no boring you, eh?—ye see today,
take today, I don't know what today's in aid of,
whether Christ was—crucified or was he—
rose fae the dead like, see what I mean?
You're an educatit man, you can tell me—
—Aye, well. There ye are. It's been seen
time and again, the working man
has nae education, he jist canny—jist

hasny got it, know what I mean,
he's jist bliddy ignorant—Christ aye,
bliddy ignorant. Well—' The bus brakes violently,
he lunges for the stair, swings down—off,
into the sun for his Easter eggs,
on very
      nearly
           steady
              legs.

Edwin Morgan

A NEGRO WOMAN

Carrying a bunch of marigolds
    wrapped
        in an old newspaper:
She carries them upright,
    bare-headed,
        the bulk
of her thighs
    causing her to waddle
        as she walks
looking into
    the store window which she passes
        on her way.
What is she
    but an ambassador
        from another world
a world of pretty marigolds
    of two shades
        which she announces
not knowing what she does
    other
        than walk the streets
holding the flowers upright
    as a torch
        so early in the morning.

William Carlos Williams

THE RETIRED COLONEL

Who lived at the top end of our street
Was a Mafeking stereotype, ageing.
Came, face pulped scarlet with kept rage,
For air past our gate.
Barked at his dog knout and whipcrack
And cowerings of India: five or six wars
Stiffened in his reddened neck;
Brow bull-down for the stroke.

Wife dead, daughters gone, lived on
Honouring his own caricature.
Shot through the heart with whisky wore
The lurch like ancient courage, would not go down
While posterity's trash stood, held
His habits like a last stand, even
As if he had Victoria rolled
In a Union Jack in that stronghold.

And what if his sort should vanish?
The rabble starlings roar upon
Trafalgar. The man-eating British lion
By a pimply age brought down.
Here's his head mounted, though only in rhymes,
Beside the head of the last English
Wolf (those starved gloomy times!)
And the last sturgeon of Thames.

Ted Hughes

OLD MEN

When there was war they went to war,
when there was peace they went to the labour exchange,
or carried hods on an hour's notice.
If their complaints were heard in Heaven
no earthly sign was given.

they have suffered obscurely a bleak recurring dream
many lifetimes long. Wounded and gassed
for noble causes they were not thought fit to understand
made idle to satisfy the greed of their betters

45

lectured when it suited the State
ignored when it suited the State
flattered by comedians
studied by young sociologists,
they have survived to be cosseted by the Regional Hospital Board.

They sit on a low stone wall in front of The Home
in an afternoon sun that shines like new,
grateful to have been allowed so much.

They puff black pipes.
Their small eyes see dead wives and children who emigrated.
They talk about the evening meal
and that old bugger George who's going senile.

When they walk in they tread gingerly,
not trusting the earth to stay beneath them for much longer.

Tony Connor

THE UNKNOWN CITIZEN

He was found by the Bureau of Statistics to be
One against whom there was no official complaint,
And all the reports on his conduct agree
That, in the modern sense of an old-fashioned word, he was a saint,
For in everything he did he served the Greater Community.
Except for the War till the day he retired
He worked in a factory and never got fired,
But satisfied his employers, Fudge Motors Inc.
Yet he wasn't a scab or odd in his views,
For his Union reports that he paid his dues,
(Our report on his Union shows it was sound)
And our Social Psychology workers found
That he was popular with his mates and liked a drink.
The Press are convinced that he bought a paper every day
And that his reactions to advertisements were normal in every way.
Policies taken out in his name prove that he was fully insured,
And his Health-card shows he was once in hospital but left it cured.

Both Producers Research and High-Grade Living declare
He was fully sensible to the advantages of the Instalment Plan

And had everything necessary to the Modern Man,
A phonograph, a radio, a car and a frigidaire.
Our researchers into Public Opinion are content
That he held the proper opinions for the time of year;
When there was peace, he was for peace; when there was war, he
went.

He was married and added five children to the population,
Which our Eugenist says was the right number for a parent of his
generation,
And our teachers report that he never interfered with their educa-
tion.
Was he free? Was he happy? The question is absurd:
Had anything been wrong, we should certainly have heard.

W.H. Auden

Members of the Family

SONNET: MOTHER LOVE

Women are always fond of growing things.
They like gardening; snipping, watering, pruning,
bringing on the backward, aware of the forward;
planting—not for nothing do they talk of 'nurseries'.
Roses are like children, a source of pride,
tulips are cosseted, primulas are pets.
These are almost as loved as the usual surrogates—
the dogs and cats that stand for families.

Conservation, preservation; it's a lovable aspect
of maternalism (one reason why we're here).
Better than that, this severe matriarchy
is established over *plants*; the bossiness, thank God,
that puts you there (delphiniums), you there (wall flowers),
is harmlessly deflected well away from us.

Gavin Ewart

MOTHER

I should be grateful. You
adopted me in a hard time,
the sound of guns from Dunkirk shaking
London, the bombs. You have told
how once you lay over my pram as a German
aeroplane swooped to machine-gun the street.
What made you, you never did say.

It was only 'You should be grateful' became
the theme you played on a subtle keyboard
(you'd not been an actress in vain):
grateful for supper, for half-days in Brighton,

for wellington boots in rainy weather,
'For all I have done for you.'
There was also your tone saying 'Don't.'

And when father left you said nothing,
except—remember?—when
I finally asked, that day in the park
at the rusted green cafeteria seats,
to distract me, 'Look at those sparrows,'
and did not notice rage boiling the dregs
of a nine-year-old's childhood away.

So I locked you from me in turn, as I locked
my schoolwork away in a case.
Where was I going? 'Out.'
And when leaving for good I came
to tell you, you carried on hanging up washing,
not taking the peg from your mouth, just said
'Remember to leave your doorkey.'

At seventy now, arthritis
has withered the touch and range
from your piano-player's hands,
your first teeth are gone (years after mine).
Hoarding a fossil faith
in Stalin, the god that failed,
you keep up the garden, read Dickens, see plays,

and we can be easier together,
and I am truly grateful.
If what you pinched and scraped once seemed
me, I know now it was for me,
understand things you still cannot say
as your talkative letters come, each signed
not 'with love,' just 'as ever'.

Andrew Waterman

THE TWO PARENTS

I love my little son, and yet when he was ill
I could not confine myself to his bedside.
I was impatient of his squalid little needs,

His laboured breathing and the fretful way he cried
And longed for my wide range of interests again,
Whereas his mother sank without another care
To that dread level of nothing but life itself
And stayed day and night, till he was better, there.

Women may pretend, yet they always dismiss
Everything but mere being just like this.

Hugh MacDiarmid

DRIVING HOME

Opposing carbeams wash my face.
Such flickerings hypnotise. To keep awake
I listen to the BBC through cracklings
of static, fade-outs under bridges,
to a cool expert who, in lower case,
computes and graphs 'the ecological
disasters that confront the human race.'

Almost immediately (ironically?),
I see blue flashing lights ahead and brake
before a car accordioned, floodlit, men heaving
at a stretcher, an ambulance oddly angled, tame, in wait.
Afterwards, silent, I drive home cautiously
where, late, the eyes of my youngest child
flicker dreamily, and are full of television.

'He's waited up,' his mother says, 'to say goodnight.'
My son smiles briefly. Such emotion! I surprise
myself and him when I hug him tight.

Dannie Abse

FARM WOMAN

She left the warmth of her body tucked round her man
before first light, for the byre, where mist and the moist
hot breath of the beasts half-hid the electric veins
of the milking machines. Later, she'd help to hoist

50

the heavy cans for the tractor to trundle down
to the farm-road end, while her raw hands scoured the dairy.
By seven o'clock, she'd have breakfast on the table,
her kitchen bright as her apron-pin, the whole house airy.

Her menfolk out in the fields, the children off to school,
she'd busy herself with house and the hens. No reasons
clouded the other side of the way she brought
to her man the generous amplitude of the seasons.

'Not much of a life', they'd whisper at church soirées
as they watched her chat, her round face buttered with content,
unable to understand that for her, each moment
rubbed out the one before, so simply lent
nothing for words of theirs to touch to argument.

Maurice Lindsay

TO MY FATHER

One of my earliest memories (remember
Those Capone hats, the polka-dot ties)
Is of the late thirties: posing
With yourself and grandfather before
The park railings; me dribbling
Ice-cream, you so spick and smiling
The congregation never imagined
How little you made. Three generations,
In the palm of a hand. A year later
Grandfather died. War was declared.

In '42 we motored to Kilmarnock
In Alec Martin's Terraplane Hudson.
We found a pond, and six goldfish
Blurred under ice. They survived
That winter, but a gull got them in the end.
Each year we picnicked on the lawn;
Mother crooking her finger
As she sipped her lime. When
They carried you out on a stretcher
She knew you'd never preach again.

51

Since you retired, we've seen more
Of each other. Yet I spend this forenoon
Typing, to bring you closer—when
We could have been together. Part of what
I dread is that clear mind nodding
Before its flickering screen. If we come over
Tonight, there will be the added irony
Of proving my visit isn't out of duty
When, to myself, I doubt the dignity
Of a love comprising so much guilt and pity.

Stewart Conn

IN MEMORY OF MY GRANDFATHER

Swearing about the weather he walked in
like an old tree and sat down;
his beard charred with tobacco, his voice
rough as the bark of his cracked hands.

Whenever he came it was the wrong time.
Roots spread over the hearth, tripped
whoever tried to move about the room;
the house was cramped with only furniture.

But I was glad of his coming. Only
through him could I breathe in the sun
and smell of fields. His clothes reeked
of the soil and the world outside;

geese and cows were the colour he made them,
he knew the language of birds and brought them
singing out of his beard, alive
to my blankets. He was winter and harvest.

Plums shone in his eyes when he rambled
of orchards. With giant thumbs he'd split
an apple through the core, and juice
flowed from his ripe, uncultured mouth.

Then, hearing the room clock chime,
he walked from my ceiling of farmyards
and returned to his forest of thunder;
the house regained silence and corners.

Slumped there in my summerless season
I longed for his rough hands and words
to break the restrictions of my bed,
to burst like a tree from my four walls.

But there was no chance again of miming
his habits or language. Only now,
years later in a cramped city, can I
be grateful for his influence and love.

Edward Storey

THE SOLITUDE OF MR POWERS

Once there was a lonely man named Mr Powers.
He was lonely because his wife fixed flowers.
Mr Powers was a gallant husband, but whenever he wished to demonstrate his gall*ant*ry
His beloved was always out with six vases and a bunch of something or other in the pantry.
He got no conversation while they ate
Because she was always nipping dead blossoms off the centrepieces and piling them on her plate.
He could get no conversation after meals because if he happened to begin one
She would look at the mantel and wonder if she shouldn't switch the small fat vase with the tall thin one.
Yes, even when she wasn't actually fixing flowers there was no forgetting about them,
Because before fixing them she was busy cutting them, and after fixing them she was fretting about them.
Mr Powers began to shave only once a week because no one cared whether his chin was scratchy;
He felt as lonely as Cavalleria without Pagliacci.
Finally he said Hey!
I might as well be alone with myself as alone with a lot of vases that have to have their water replenished every day,
And he walked off into the dawn,
And his wife just kept on refilling vases and never noticed that he was gone.
Beware of floral arrangements;
They lead to marital estrangements.

Ogden Nash

The aunts who knew not Africa
But spoke of having been to Weymouth in the spring—
Not last spring but the year the lilac was so good—
Who never saw prize-fighters in a ring,
But could recall a fox-hunt in the neighbourhood.

Two aunts who never went abroad,
Nor travelled far in love, nor were much wronged, nor sinned
A lot—but for such peccadillos as to damn,
With tiny oaths, late frost or some chill wind,
Slugs at the dahlias or wasps at homemade jam.

Two aunts who, after silences,
Spoke knowingly of angels passing overhead;
But who prayed little and slept well, were worried less
By death than weeds: but hoped to die in bed,
Untouched by magic or by economic stress.

This age's beneficiaries
For whom our century endows this box of dreams,
Conferring prize-fighters, dancers of unimaginable grace,
Glimpses of Africa, of football teams,
Of statesmen, of the finish of a classic race.

Vestals of the impalpable,
Dazed by its prodigality, by acrobats
On bicycles, by lovers speaking Shakespeare's lines,
Mazed by murders, by speeches from democrats,
Wooed by cooking hints and the Paris dress designs.

Flirt on, soft spinsters, flirt with time.
Order the crowded hours, vicariously tranced.
Know Africa and judge which prize-fighter was hurt,
How well the latest ballerina danced,
How cake, or love, was made. O flirt, my two aunts, flirt!

John Pudney

THE DEATH OF AUNT ALICE

Aunt Alice's funeral was orderly,
each mourner correct, dressed in decent black,
not one balding relative berserk with an axe.
Poor Alice, where's your opera-ending?
For alive you relished high catastrophe,
your bible Page One of a newspaper.

You talked of typhoid when we sat to eat;
Fords on the M4, mangled, upside down,
just when we were going for a spin;
and, at London airport, as you waved us off,
how you fatigued us with 'metal fatigue',
vague shapes of Boeings bubbling under seas.

Such disguises and such transformations!
Even trees were but factories for coffins,
rose bushes decoys to rip boys' eyes with thorns.
Sparrows became vampires, spiders had designs,
and your friends also grew SPECTACULAR,
none to bore you by dying naturally.

A. had both kidneys removed in error
at Guy's. 'And such a clever surgeon too.'
B., one night, fell screaming down a liftshaft.
'Poor fellow, he never had a head for heights.'
C., so witty, so feminine, 'Pity
she ended up in a concrete-mixer.'

But now, never again, Alice, will you utter
gory admonitions as some do oaths.
Disasters that lit your eyes will no more
unless, trembling up there, pale saints listen
to details of their bloody martyrdoms,
all their tall stories, your eternity.

Dannie Abse

Once more the storm is howling, and half hid
Under this cradle-hood and coverlid
My child sleeps on. There is no obstacle
But Gregory's wood and one bare hill
Whereby the haystack- and roof-levelling wind,
Bred on the Atlantic, can be stayed;
And for an hour I have walked and prayed
Because of the great gloom that is in my mind.

I have walked and prayed for this young child an hour
And heard the sea-wind scream upon the tower.
And under the arches of the bridge, and scream
In the elms above the flooded stream;
Imagining in excited reverie
That the future years had come,
Dancing to a frenzied drum,
Out of the murderous innocence of the sea.

May she be granted beauty and yet not
Beauty to make a stranger's eye distraught
Or hers before a looking-glass, for such,
Being made beautiful overmuch,
Consider beauty a sufficient end,
Lose natural kindness and maybe
The heart-revealing intimacy
That chooses right, and never find a friend.

Helen being chosen found life flat and dull
And later had much trouble from a fool,
While that great Queen, that rose from out of the spray,
Being fatherless could have her way
Yet chose a bandy-legged smith for man.
It's certain that fine women eat
A crazy salad with their meat
Whereby the Horn of Plenty is undone.

In courtesy I'd have her chiefly learned;
Hearts are not had as a gift but hearts are earned
By those that are not entirely beautiful;
Yet many, that have played the fool
For beauty's very self, has charm made wise,
And many a poor man that has roved,

Loved and thought himself beloved,
From a glad kindness cannot take his eyes.

May she become a flourishing hidden tree
That all her thoughts may like the linnet be,
And have no business but dispensing round
Their magnanimities of sound,
Nor but in merriment begin a chase,
Nor but in merriment a quarrel.
O may she live like some green laurel
Rooted to one dear perpetual place.

My mind, because the minds that I have loved,
The sort of beauty that I have approved,
Prosper but little, has dried up of late,
Yet knows that to be choked with hate
May well be of all evil chances chief.
If there's no hatred in a mind
Assault and battery of the wind
Can never tear the linnet from the leaf.

An intellectual hatred is the worst,
So let her think opinions are accursed.
Have I not seen the loveliest woman born
Out of the mouth of Plenty's horn,
Because of her opinionated mind
Barter that horn and every good
By quiet natures understood
For an old bellows full of angry wind?

Considering that, all hatred driven hence,
The soul recovers radical innocence
And learns at last that it is self-delighting,
Self-appeasing, self-affrighting,
And that its own sweet will is Heaven's will;
She can, though every face should scowl
And every windy quarter howl
Or every bellows burst, be happy still.

And may her bridegroom bring her to a house
Where all's accustomed, ceremonious;
For arrogance and hatred are the wares
Peddled in the thoroughfares.
How but in custom and in ceremony

Are innocence and beauty born?
Ceremony's a name for the rich horn,
And custom for the spreading laurel tree.

W. B. Yeats

TARKINGTON, THOU SHOULDST BE LIVING IN THIS HOUR

O Adolescence, O Adolescence,
I wince before thine incandescence.
Thy constitution young and hearty
Is too much for this aged party.
Thou standest with loafer-flattened feet
Where bras and funny papers meet.
When anxious elders swarm about
Crying 'Where are you going?' thou answerest 'Out',
Leaving thy parents swamped in debts
For bubble-gum and cigarettes.

Thou spurnest in no uncertain tone
The sirloin for the ice-cream cone;
Not milk, but cola, is thy potion;
Thou wearest earrings in the ocean,
Blue jeans at dinner, or maybe shorts,
And lipstick on the tennis courts.

For ever thou whisperest, two by two,
Of who is madly in love with who.
The car thou needest every day,
Let hub caps scatter where they may.
For it would start unfriendly talk
If friends should chance to see thee walk.

Friends! Heavens, how they come and go!
Best pal today, tomorrow foe,
Since to distinguish thou dost fail
'Twixt confidante and tattletale,
And blanchest to find the beach at noon
With sacred midnight secrets strewn.

Strewn! All is lost and nothing found.
Lord, how thou leavest things around!
Sweaters and rackets in the stable,

And purse upon the drugstore table,
And cameras rusting in the rain,
And Daddy's patience down the drain.

Ah well, I must not carp and cavil,
I'll chew the spinach, spit out the gravel,
Remembering how my heart has leapt
At times when me thou didst accept.
Still, I'd like to be present, I must confess,
When thine own adolescents adolesce.

Ogden Nash

THIS IS JUST TO SAY

I have eaten
the plums
that were in
the icebox

and which
you were probably
saving
for breakfast

Forgive me
they were delicious
so sweet
and so cold

William Carlos Williams

THE RETURN

Four days we did not speak, tried to pretend
This time we'd bring this marriage to an end,
Consulting train timetables, considering where
We could divide our chattels, share by share,
Correcting our 'ours', biting our lips on 'we',
Calling this house 'mine', expounding bitterly
Who should leave whom, with whom the children should
Stay, until it seemed as if this time had come for good,
The break had come. Neither could humble pride,

Mollify hate, come timidly confessing wrong.
The days dragged slowly harrowing along,
The nights all tautness in our limbs and ears,
Broken with fugitive retreats, uneasy fears.
Meanwhile you blossomed womanly, a brightening crown
Brushed in your hair, dress shoulder would slip down,
Painted your toes, you moved your hips in poise
Making our home shine, filling the place with noise,
Piano-preludes, stories for the children, dust
Flying woebegone, laundry line-tossed,
Then again in basketfuls come sweet and dry
While swirl the willow skirts and the uncertain summer sky
Throws lights across your polished floors and our
Home patterns. Now I cease to glower
My fit reverts to its original anxiety, and then
Turns to destructive: I shout at you again
And as this leaves my lips I hear the cold echo
Of a man left alone between these walls, and know
How much I love you, suddenly, like a pulled tendon, taut
Runs the touched nerve. I can see that you are hurt,
And yet I will not humble me: as I pass by
Silent, withdrawn, my belly heaves, heart gives a sigh
My body wrestles like a captive in a net,
Heart, mind, compassion fight me strenuously, yet:
I dare not let them free. Until you lift the phone,
And I must plead for amnesty. Bruised, in a stun
Our day goes by, then the return of trust
Restores romantic softnesses, that rise away to lust.

I watched the water spring this morning wondering
At its continual fullness as each ripple ring
Spread from the source, at the continual wave
That wells restoring by such waterlights. The peace you gave
Flows thus back round our home: in this fresh lake
Our children dance, the blue kingfisher streaks, the waterflowers
   awake.

David Holbrook

AN ADDITION TO THE FAMILY: FOR M.L.

A musical poet, collector of basset-horns,
was buttering his toast down in Dumbartonshire
when suddenly from behind the breakfast newspaper

the shining blade stopped scraping
and he cried to his wife, 'Joyce, listen to this!—
"Two basset-hounds for sale, house-trained, keen hunters"—
Oh we must have them! What d'you think?' 'But dear,
did you say *hounds*?' 'Yes Yes, hounds, hounds—'
'But Maurice, it's *horns* we want, you must be over
in the livestock column, you can't play a hound!'
'It's Beverley it says, the kennels are at Beverley—'
'But Maurice—' '—I'll get some petrol, we'll be there by
    lunchtime—'
'But a dog, two dogs, where'll we put them?'
'I've often wondered what these dogs are like—'
'You mean you don't even—' 'Is there no more marmalade?'
'—don't know what they look like? And how are we to feed them?
Yes, there's the pot dear.' 'This stuff's all peel, isn't it?'
'Well, we're at the end of it. But look, these two great—'
'You used to make marmalade once upon a time.'
'They've got ears down to here, and they're far too—'
'Is that half past eight? I'll get the car out.
See if I left my cheque-book on the —' 'Maurice,
are you mad? What about your horns?' 'What horns,
what are you talking about? Look Joyce dear,
if it's not on the dresser it's in my other jacket.
I believe they're wonderful for rabbits—'
So the musical poet took his car to Beverley
with his wife and his cheque-book, and came back home
with his wife and his cheque-book and two new hostages
to the unexpectedness of fortune.
The creatures scampered through the grass, the children
came out with cries of joy, there seemed to be nothing
dead or dying in all that landscape.
Fortune bless the unexpected cries!
Life gathers to the point of wishing it,
a mocking pearl of many ventures. The house
rolled on its back and kicked its legs in the air.
And later, wondering farmers as they passed would hear
behind the lighted window in the autumn evening
two handsome mellow-bosomed basset-hounds
howling to a melodious basset-horn.

Edwin Morgan

Love

SYMPTOMS OF LOVE

Love is a universal migraine,
A bright stain on the vision
Blotting out reason.

Symptoms of true love
Are leanness, jealousy,
Laggard dawns;

Are omens and nightmares—
Listening for a knock,
Waiting for a sign:

For a touch of her fingers
In a darkened room,
For a searching look.

Take courage, lover!
Can you endure such grief
At any hand but hers?

Robert Graves

STRAWBERRIES

There were never strawberries
like the ones we had
that sultry afternoon
sitting on the step
of the open french window
facing each other
your knees held in mine

the blue plates in our laps
the strawberries glistening
in the hot sunlight
we dipped them in sugar
looking at each other
not hurrying the feast
for one to come
the empty plates
laid on the stone together
with the two forks crossed
and I bent towards you
sweet in that air
in my arms
abandoned like a child
from your eager mouth
the taste of strawberries
in my memory
lean back again
let me love you
let the sun beat
on our forgetfulness
one hour of all
the heat intense
and summer lightning
on the Kilpatrick hills

let the storm wash the plates

Edwin Morgan

MY FIRST SWEETHEART

You were the belle of the street
And very conscious of it.
You were a shade richer
Than everyone else and knew
In your bones you were better
Than those of us who danced
Outside your main door,
Coming from flats, where
Darkness was thicker
Than thin air, so you stood

Outside the grand door and let
Us have just a squint inside.
You never deigned to play with us,
Displayed inordinate pride,
Mocked our clumsiness,
Our coarse voices, our
School uniforms labelling us
As lesser beings than you.
But I loved you and
I didn't understand what love was
For or how you did it.
I just loved you, and
I wonder if you remember
A valentine that had on it
The outline of a hand,
A pink water-colour wash,
And the words 'I love you'
Written all over it?
I sent that. I posted it
Myself and walked past
Your house for a sign
That you had seen it
And had understood.
But nothing happened.
The world didn't suddenly become
Marvellous for me, my life
Didn't really alter. So
I'll remember you in
Your golden ringlets, in
Your party dresses
That I saw sometimes passing
By your house. Your
Plump cheeks will always
Signify something transcendental
For me. I wonder what became
Of you when you left the street,
Left me without anything substantial
To dream about, with your house
Become a bed-and-breakfast place.
The light steps that took me round
The corner to see you became slow
And I scuffed my satchel in the
Leaves as they gathered outside
Your door. But it wasn't the same

Without you. You must have
Been the same age as me.
Seven or eight or nine.
Still, I don't think anyone
Has ever been so mysterious.
Of course, we'll never meet.
These things never really happen.
Perhaps just as well.
Though I wonder what would
Have happened if I had just once
Come and pulled your bell
And said: 'Hello, I love you.'

Alan Bold

TWICE SHY

Her scarf *à la* Bardot,
In suede flats for the walk,
She came with me one evening
For air and friendly talk.
We crossed the quiet river,
Took the embankment walk.

Traffic holding its breath,
Sky a tense diaphragm:
Dusk hung like a backcloth
That shook where a swan swam,
Tremulous as a hawk
Hanging deadly, calm.

A vacuum of need
Collapsed each hunting heart
But tremulously we held
As hawk and prey apart,
Preserved classic decorum,
Deployed our talk with art.

Our juvenilia
Had taught us both to wait,
Not to publish feeling
And regret it all too late—
Mushroom loves already
Had puffed and burst in hate.

So, chary and excited
As a thrush linked on a hawk,
We thrilled to the March twilight
With nervous childish talk:
Still waters running deep
Along the embankment walk.

Seamus Heaney

O THE VALLEY IN THE SUMMER

O the valley in the summer where I and my John
Beside the deep river would walk on and on
While the flowers at our feet and the birds up above
Argued so sweetly on reciprocal love,
And I leaned on his shoulder; 'O Johnny, Let's play';
But he frowned like thunder and he went away.

O that Friday near Christmas as I well recall
When we went to the Charity Matinée Ball,
The floor was so smooth and the band was so loud
And Johnny so handsome I felt so proud;
'Squeeze me tighter, dear Johnny, Let's dance till it's day';
But he frowned like thunder and he went away.

Shall I ever forget at the Grand Opera
When music poured out of each wonderful star?
Diamonds and pearls they hung dazzling down
Over each silver or golden silk gown;
'O John I'm in heaven,' I whispered to say:
But he frowned like thunder and he went away.

O but he was as fair as a garden in flower,
As slender and tall as the great Eiffel Tower,
When the waltz throbbed out on the long promenade
O his eyes and his smile they went straight to my heart;
'O marry me, Johnny, I'll love and obey':
But he frowned like thunder and he went away.

O last night I dreamed of you, Johnny, my lover,
You'd the sun on one arm and the moon on the other,
The sea it was blue and the grass it was green,

Every star rattled a round tambourine;
Ten thousand miles deep in a pit there I lay:
But you frowned like thunder and you went away.

W. H. Auden

NIGHT RIDE

Swiftly the black
leather strap
of the night
deserted road

on rolls the freighted
lurching bus.
Huddled together
two lovers doze

their hands linked
across their laps
their bodies loosely
interlocked

their heads resting
two heavy fruits
on the plaited
basket of their limbs.

Slowly the bus
slides into light.
Here are hills
detached from dark

the road uncoils
a white ribbon
the lovers with
the hills unfold

wake cold
to face the fate
of those who love
despite the world.

Herbert Read

A SUBALTERN'S LOVE-SONG

Miss J. Hunter Dunn, Miss J. Hunter Dunn,
Furnish'd and burnish'd by Aldershot sun,
What strenuous singles we played after tea,
We in the tournament—you against me!

Love-thirty, love-forty, oh! weakness of joy,
The speed of a swallow, the grace of a boy,
With carefullest carelessness, gaily you won,
I am weak from your loveliness, Joan Hunter Dunn.

Miss Joan Hunter Dunn, Miss Joan Hunter Dunn,
How mad I am, sad I am, glad that you won.
The warm-handled racket is back in its press,
But my shock-headed victor, she loves me no less.

Her father's euonymus shines as we walk,
And swing past the summer-house, buried in talk,
And cool the verandah that welcomes us in
To the six-o'clock news and a lime-juice and gin.

The scent of the conifers, sound of the bath,
The view from my bedroom of moss-dappled path,
As I struggle with double-end evening tie,
For we dance at the Golf Club, my victor and I.

On the floor of her bedroom lie blazer and shorts
And the cream-coloured walls are be-trophied with sports,
And westering, questioning settles the sun
On your low-leaded window, Miss Joan Hunter Dunn.

The Hillman is waiting, the light's in the hall,
The pictures of Egypt are bright on the wall,
My sweet, I am standing beside the oak stair
And there on the landing's the light on your hair.

By roads 'not adopted', by woodlanded ways,
She drove to the club in the late summer haze,
Into nine-o'clock Camberley, heavy with bells
And mushroomy, pine-woody, evergreen smells.

Miss Joan Hunter Dunn, Miss Joan Hunter Dunn,
I can hear from the car-park the dance has begun.

Oh! full Surrey twilight! importunate band!
Oh! strongly adorable tennis-girl's hand!

Around us are Rovers and Austins afar,
Above us, the intimate roof of the car,
And here on my right is the girl of my choice,
With the tilt of her nose and the chime of her voice,

And the scent of her wrap, and the words never said,
And the ominous, ominous dancing ahead.
We sat in the car park till twenty to one
And now I'm engaged to Miss Joan Hunter Dunn.

John Betjeman

WEDDING-WIND

The wind blew all my wedding-day,
And my wedding-night was the night of the high wind;
And a stable door was banging, again and again,
That he must go and shut it, leaving me
Stupid in candlelight, hearing rain,
Seeing my face in the twisted candlestick,
Yet seeing nothing. When he came back
He said the horses were restless, and I was sad
That any man or beast that night should lack
The happiness I had.

                    Now in the day
All's ravelled under the sun by the wind's blowing.
He has gone to look at the floods, and I
Carry a chipped pail to the chicken-run,
Set it down, and stare. All is the wind
Hunting through clouds and forests, thrashing
My apron and the hanging cloths on the line.
Can it be borne, this bodying-forth by wind
Of joy my actions turn on, like a thread
Carrying beads? Shall I be let to sleep
Now this perpetual morning shares my bed?
Can even death dry up
These new delighted lakes, conclude
Our kneeling as cattle by all-generous waters?

Philip Larkin

THE RIVER-MERCHANT'S WIFE: A LETTER

While my hair was still cut straight across my forehead
I played about the front gate, pulling flowers.
You came by on bamboo stilts, playing horse,
You walked about my seat, playing with blue plums.
And we went on living in the village of Chokan:
Two small people, without dislike or suspicion.

At fourteen I married My Lord—you.
I never laughed, being bashful.
Lowering my head, I looked at the wall.
Called to, a thousands times, I never looked back.

At fifteen I stopped scowling.
I desired my dust to be mingled with yours
Forever and forever and forever.
Why should I climb the look-out?

At sixteen you departed,
You went into far Ku-to-yen, by the river of swirling eddies,
And you have been gone five months.
The monkeys make sorrowful noise overhead.

You dragged your feet when you went out.
By the gate now, the moss is grown, the different mosses,
Too deep to clear them away!
The leaves fall early this Autumn, in wind.
The paired butterflies are already yellow with August
Over the grass in the West garden;
They hurt me. I grow older.
If you are coming down through the narrows of the river Kiang,
Please let me know beforehand,
And I will come out to meet you
                    As far as Cho-fu-sa.

translated from the Chinese by
Ezra Pound

GOODBYE

So we must say Goodbye, my darling,
And go, as lovers go, for ever;
Tonight remains, to pack and fix on labels
And make an end of lying down together.

I put a final shilling in the gas,
And watch you slip your dress below your knees
And lie so still I hear your rustling comb
Modulate the autumn in the trees.

And all the countless things I shall remember
Lay mummy-cloths of silence round my head;
I fill the carafe with a drink of water;
You say 'We paid a guinea for this bed,'

And then, 'We'll leave some gas, a little warmth
For the next resident, and these dry flowers,'
And turn your face away, afraid to speak
The big word, that Eternity is ours.

Your kisses close my eyes and yet you stare
As though God struck a child with nameless fears;
Perhaps the water flitters and discloses
Time's chalice and its limpid useless tears.

Everything we renounce except ourselves;
Selfishness is the last of all to go;
Our sighs are exhalations of the earth,
Our footprints leave a track across the snow.

We made the universe to be our home,
Our nostrils took the wind to be our breath,
Our hearts are massive towers of delight,
We stride across the seven seas of death.

Yet when all's done you'll keep the emerald
I placed upon your finger in the street;
And I will keep the patches that you sewed
On my old battledress tonight, my sweet.

Alun Lewis

ABSENCE

I visited the place where we last met.
Nothing was changed, the gardens were well-tended,
The fountains sprayed their usual steady jet;
There was no sign that anything had ended
And nothing to instruct me to forget.

The thoughtless birds that shook out of the trees,
Singing an ecstasy I could not share,
Played cunning in my thoughts. Surely in these
Pleasures there could not be a pain to bear
Or any discord shake the level breeze.

It was because the place was just the same
That made your absence seem a savage force,
For under all the gentleness there came
An earthquake tremor: fountain, birds and grass
Were shaken by my thinking of your name.

Elizabeth Jennings

NOT AT HOME

Her house loomed at the end of a Berkshire lane,
Tall but retired. She was expecting me;
And I approached with light heart and quick tread,
Having already seen from the garden gate
How bright her knocker shone—in readiness
For my confident rap?—and the steps holystoned.
I ran the last few paces, rapped and listened
Intently for the rustle of her approach . . . .

No reply, no movement. I waited three long minutes,
Then, in surprise, went down the path again
To observe the chimney stacks. No smoke from either.
And the curtains: were they drawn against the sun?
Or against what, then? I glanced over a wall
At her well-tended orchard, heavy with bloom
(Easter fell late that year, Spring had come early)
And found the gardener, bent over cold frames.

'Her ladyship is not at home?'
                              'No, sir.'
'She was expecting me. My name is Lyon.
Did she leave a note?'
                              'No, sir, she left no note.'
'I trust nothing has happened . . . ?'
                              'No, sir, nothing . . . .
And yet she seemed preoccupied: we guess
Some family reason.'
                              '*Has* she a family?'
'That, sir, I could not say . . . . She seemed distressed—
Not quite herself, if I may venture so.'
'But she left no note?'
                              'Only a verbal message:
Her ladyship will be away some weeks
Or months, hopes to return before midsummer,
And, please, you are not to communicate.
There was something else: about the need for patience.'

The sun went in, a bleak wind shook the blossom,
Dust flew, the windows glared in a blank row . . . .
And yet I felt, when I turned slowly away,
Her eyes boring my back, as it might be posted
Behind a curtain slit, and still in love.

Robert Graves

A SLICE OF WEDDING CAKE

Why have such scores of lovely, gifted girls
    Married impossible men?
Simple self-sacrifice may be ruled out,
    And missionary endeavour, nine times out of ten.

Repeat 'impossible men': not merely rustic,
    Foul-tempered or depraved
(Dramatic foils chosen to show the world
    How well women behave, and always have behaved).

Impossible men: idle, illiterate,
    Self-pitying, dirty, sly,
For whose appearance even in City parks
    Excuses must be made to casual passers-by.

Has God's supply of tolerable husbands
  Fallen, in fact, so low?
Or do I always over-value woman
  At the expense of man?
                Do I?
                  It might be so.

Robert Graves

Sports and Recreations

THE GAME

Follow the crowds to where the turnstiles click.
The terraces fill. *Hoompa*, blares the brassy band.
Saturday afternoon has come to Ninian Park
and, beyond the goalposts, in the Canton Stand
between black spaces, a hundred matches spark.

Waiting, we recall records, legendary scores:
Fred Keenor, Hardy, in a royal blue shirt.
The very names, sad as the old songs, open doors
before our time where someone else was hurt.
Now, like an injured beast, the great crowd roars.

The coin is spun. Here all is simplified
and we are partisan who cheer the Good,
hiss at passing Evil. Was Lucifer offside?
A wing falls down when cherubs howl for blood.
Demons have agents: the Referee is bribed.

The white ball smacked the crossbar. Satan rose
higher than the others in the smoked brown gloom
to sink on grass in a ballet dancer's pose.
Again, it seems, we hear a familiar tune
not quite identifiable. A distant whistle blows.

Memory of faded games, the discarded years;
talk of Aston Villa, Orient, and the Swans.
Half-time, the band played the same military airs
as when The Bluebirds once were champions.
Round touchlines the same cripples in their chairs.

Mephistopheles had his joke. The honest team
dribbles ineffectually, no one can be blamed.
Infernal backs tackle, inside forwards scheme,

and if they foul us need we be ashamed?
Heads up! Oh for a Ted Drake, a Dixie Dean.

'Saved' or else, discontents, we are transferred
long decades back, like Faust must pay that fee.
The Night is early. Great phantoms in us stir
as coloured jerseys hover, move diagonally
on the damp turf, and our eidetic visions blur.

God sign our souls! Because the obscure Staff
of Hell rule this world, jugular fans guessed
the result half-way through the second half
and those who know the score just seem depressed.
Small boys swarm the field for an autograph.

Silent the Stadium. The crowds have all filed out.
Only the pigeons beneath the roofs remain.
The clean programmes are trampled underfoot
and natural the dark, appropriate the rain
whilst, under lamp-posts, threatening newsboys shout.

Dannie Abse

CRICKET AT WORCESTER 1938

Dozing in deck-chair's gentle curve,
Through half-closed eyes I watched the cricket,
Knowing the sporting press would say
'Perks bowled well on a perfect wicket.'

Fierce mid-day sun upon the ground,
Through heat-haze came the hollow sound
Of wary bat on ball, to pound
The devil from it, quell its bound.

Sunburned fieldsmen, flannelled cream,
Seemed, though urgent, scarce alive,
Swooped, like swallows of a dream
On skimming fly, the hard-hit drive.

Beyond the score-box, through the trees
Gleamed Severn, blue and wide,
Where oarsmen 'feathered' with polished ease
And passed in gentle glide.

The back-cloth, setting off the setting,
Peter's cathedral soared,
Rich of shade and fine of fretting,
Like cut and painted board.

To the cathedral, close for shelter,
Huddled houses, bent and slim,
Some tall, some short, all helter-skelter,
Like a sky-line drawn for Grimm.

This the fanciful engraver might
In his creative dream have seen—
Here, framed by summer's glaring light—
Grey stone, majestic over green.

Closer, the bowler's arm swept down,
The ball swung, pitched and darted;
Stump and bail flashed and flew;
The batsman pensively departed.

Like rattle of dry seeds in pods
The warm crowd faintly clapped—
The boys who came to watch their gods,
The tired old men who napped.

The members sat in their strong deck-chairs
And sometimes glanced at the play,
They smoked and talked of stocks and shares,
And the bar stayed open all day.

John Arlott

CRICKET AT SWANSEA
(Glamorgan in the Field)

From the top of the hill-top pavilion,
The sea is a cheat to the eye,
Where it secretly seeps into coastline
Or fades in the fellow-grey sky;
But the crease-marks are sharp on the green
As the axe's first taste of the tree,
And keen is the Welshmen's assault
As the freshening fret from the sea.

The ball is a withering weapon,
Fraught with a strong-fingered spin
And the fieldsmen, with fingers prehensile,
Are the arms of attack moving in.
In the field of a new Cymric mission,
With outcricket cruel as a cat
To pounce on the perilous snick
As it flicks from the break-harried bat.

On this turf, the remembered of rugby—
'The Invincibles'—came by their name,
And now, in the calm of the clubhouse,
Frown down from their old-fashioned frame.
Their might has outlived their moustaches,
For photos fade faster than fame;
And this cricket rekindles the temper
Of their high-trampling, scrummaging game:
Intense as an Eisteddfod anthem
It burns down the day like a flame.

John Arlott

MILLOM CRICKET FIELD

Let me first describe the field:
Its size, a double acre; walled
Along the north by a schoolyard,
West by a hedge and orchards; tarred
Wood railings on the east to fence
The grass from the station shunting lines,
That crook like a defensive ditch
Below the ramparts of the church;
And south, the butter meadows, yellow
As fat and bumpy as a pillow,
Rumpling down the mile or more
That slopes to the wide Cumbrian shore,
With not a brick to lift a ban
Between the eye and the Isle of Man.
A common sort of field you'll say:
You'd find a dozen any day
In any northern town, a sour
Flat landscape shaped with weed and wire,
And nettle clump and ragwort thicket—

But this field is put by for cricket.
Here among the grass and plantains
Molehills matter more than mountains,
And generations watch the score
Closer than toss of peace or war.
Here, in matches won and lost,
The town hoards an heroic past,
And legendary bowlers tie
The child's dream in the father's lie.
This is no Wisden pitch; no place
For classic cuts and Newbolt's verse,
But the luck of the league, stiff and stark
With animosity of dark
In-grown village and mining town,
When evening smoke—light drizzles down,
And the fist is tight in the trouser pocket,
And the heart turns black for the want of a wicket.

Or knock-out cricket, brisk as a bird,
Twenty overs and league men barred—
Heels in the popping crease, crouch and clout.
And the crowd half-codding the batsman out.
Over the thorn and elder hedge
The sunlight floods, but leaves a ledge
Of shadow where the old men sit,
Dozing their pipes out. Frays of light
Seam a blue serge suit; gnats swarm,
And swallows dip round the bowler's arm.
Here in a small-town game is seen
The long-linked dance of the village green:
Wishing well and maypole ring,
Mumming and ritual of spring.

Norman Nicholson

HUNTER TRIALS

It's awf'lly bad luck on Diana,
   Her ponies have swallowed their bits;
She fished down their throats with a spanner
   And frightened them all into fits.

So now she's attempting to borrow.
  Do lend her some bits, Mummy, *do*;
I'll lend her my own for tomorrow,
  But today *I'll* be wanting them too.

Just look at Prunella on Guzzle,
  The wizardest pony on earth;
Why doesn't she slacken his muzzle
  And tighten the breech in his girth?

I say, Mummy, there's Mrs Geyser
  And doesn't she look pretty sick?
I bet it's because Mona Lisa
  Was hit on the hock with a brick.

Miss Blewitt says Monica threw it,
  But Monica says it was Joan,
And Joan's very thick with Miss Blewitt,
  So Monica's sulking alone.

And Margaret failed in her paces,
  Her withers got tied in a noose,
So her coronet's caught in the traces
  And now all her fetlocks are loose.

Oh, it's me now. I'm terribly nervous.
  I wonder if Smudges will shy.
She's practically certain to swerve as
  Her Pelham is over one eye.

           *   *   *

Oh wasn't it naughty of Smudges?
  Oh, Mummy, I'm sick with disgust.
She threw me in front of the Judges,
  And my silly old collarbone's bust.

John Betjeman

THE SURF-RIDER

Out in the Golfe de Gascogne, on the far
edge of the Atlantic beside Biarritz,
the surf-rider surfaces from a trough

in the sea's swell, seeming to pull at the reins
of air currents while the wave wheels him
as on a chariot, the horses of momentum,
harnessed to wind, throwing back manes of sea-spray:

When the wave's swelling explodes in a dust-
storm of surf with a crowd-roar in the bay's
amphitheatre of tiers of the tide's coming,
he wobbles a moment as in a rut, then,
leaning into the wind, arms loosening,
makes the surf as firm as cobblestones, his
heels as secure as iron rims on wheels:

And now he rides the ocean, conqueror
of air and water in a contest of force,
heeling above the lion's pit of depth:
until the surf eases, reaches the shore,
dragging him down to his knees. The illusion,
that a god has risen from the ocean
and miraculously walked upon water, breaks.

                                        Zulfikar Ghose

SHEEPDOG TRIALS IN HYDE PARK

A shepherd stands at one end of the arena.
Five sheep are unpenned at the other. His dog runs out
In a curve to behind them, fetches them straight to the shepherd,
Then drives the flock round a triangular course
Through a couple of gates and back to his master; two
Must be sorted there from the flock, then all five penned.
Gathering, driving away, shedding and penning
Are the plain words for the miraculous game.

An abstract game. What can the sheepdog make of such
Simplified terrain?—no hills, dales, bogs, walls, tracks,
Only a quarter-mile plain of grass, dumb crowds
Like crowds on hoardings around it, and behind them
Traffic or mounds of lovers and children playing.
Well, the dog is no landscape-fancier; his whole concern
Is with his master's whistle, and of course
With the flock—sheep are sheep anywhere for him.

The sheep are the chanciest element. Why, for instance,
Go through this gate when there's on either side of it
No wall or hedge but huge and viable space?
Why not eat the grass instead of being pushed around it?
Like blobs of quicksilver on a tilting board
The flock erratically runs, dithers, breaks up,
Is reassembled: their ruling idea is the dog;
And behind the dog, though they know it not yet, is a shepherd.

The shepherd knows that time is of the essence
But haste calamitous. Between dog and sheep
There is always an ideal distance, a perfect angle;
But these are constantly varying, so the man
Should anticipate each move through the dog, his medium.
The shepherd is the brain behind the dog's brain,
But his control of dog, like dog's of sheep,
Is never absolute—that's the beauty of it.

For beautiful it is. The guided missiles,
The black-and-white angels follow each quirk and jink of
The evasive sheep, play grandmother's steps behind them,
Freeze to the ground, or leap to head off a straggler
Almost before it knows that it wants to stray,
As if radar-controlled. But they are not machines—
You can feel them feeling mastery, doubt, chagrin:
Machines don't frolic when their job is done.

What's needfully done in the solitude of sheep-runs—
Those tough, real tasks—becomes this stylized game,
A demonstration of intuitive wit
Kept natural by the saving grace of error.
To lift, to fetch, to drive, to shed, to pen
Are acts I recognize, with all they mean
Of shepherding the unruly, for a kind of
Controlled woolgathering is my work too.

C. Day Lewis

PIGEON COTES ON PENISTONE ROAD, SHEFFIELD

Past where a complex of multi-storey flats
Fences off the view from terraced houses
And above Weir Head where, jammed on stones,

The larger rubbish cordons off the smaller rubbish
From the lower river, a dozen pigeon cotes
Painted football colours stand in clearings
Among the willow herb. This Sunday morning
The pigeons, tethered by instinct and safe in the valley
As a match between cupped hands from the wind,
Crisscross their wings on the air. I remember my Father's
Fostering homers beaten down by a storm
And Uncle Tom's being turbaned with glory
From winning the Federation from San Sebastian.
Sometimes to someone pigeon fanciers,
Backyard mechanics, rabbit breeders,
Hermit chrysanthemum growers on allotments
And trumpet players in silver prize bands
Are/were/will be great.

Stanley Cook

THE DIVER

Poised for the leap, clear in the morning light
He falls through flashing space
In one swift curve of flight;
A moment when he seems to pause and wait,
Then like an arrow rives the depths—
Soundless the waters close.
The tumult of the sea to fill his ears,
The touch of smooth slim fingers, soft and cool,
That mould the rippling waters to his shape,
As he moves onward with unswerving flight
Through the dim silence of a hidden world
Of strange quick light and shade;
Down quivering depths of clear, cold, frigid green,
Stray gleams of sunlight and deep purple gloom.
Upwards at last, he thrusts from out the deep,
With strong defiant shake, to fling
The salt spray from his eyes. White gleaming arms
That rise and fall, and beat the waves to live.
Strongly he breasts the sea, towards the rising sun.
The morning light.

Theobald Purcell-Buret

SEASIDE GOLF

How straight it flew, how long it flew,
  It clear'd the rutty track
And soaring, disappeared from view
  Beyond the bunker's back—
A glorious, sailing, bounding drive
That made me glad I was alive.

And down the fairway, far along
  It glowed a lonely white;
I played an iron sure and strong
  And clipp'd it out of sight,
And spite of grassy banks between
I knew I'd find it on the green.

And so I did. It lay content
  Two paces from the pin;
A steady putt and then it went
  Oh, most securely in.
The very turf rejoiced to see
That quite unprecedented three.

Ah! seaweed smells from sandy caves
  And thyme and mist in whiffs,
In-coming tide, Atlantic waves
  Slapping the sunny cliffs,
Lark song and sea sounds in the air
And splendour, splendour everywhere.

John Betjeman

INDOOR SPORTS

Darts

Begin and end with a double. He places his feet
Square apart on the rubber mat. I bet I shall end
As always on double one. The squeaking chalk
Subtracts, subtracts . . . What did I tell you? And why
Is it the hardest bed? Singles are useless
And there is no going back.
                          He flicks his wrist,
Hardly looking, and wins.

Shove halfpenny

On the field of elm or slate the lines are far too close;
The brass discs knock each other out of place.
You need a glancing blow with the ball of the thumb;
One disc can knock another one into place
With skill and join her there. No, not like that;
Like this.
       You see. Both safely between the lines.
With skill, as I said. And luck.

Vingt-et-un

Stay, twist, or buy. Ace is eleven or one.
Not really much scope for skill, I could play this game in my sleep:
Still, talking of sleep, it too can pass the time.
Yes, what do you think? I'm going for five and under;
I ought to twist but I'll buy.
       The small cards fall;
I'm buying again, I ought to be bust, but there—
It paid me not to twist!

Crossword puzzles

Ninety-nine down: a one-letter word meaning something indefi-
nite.
The indefinite article or—would it perhaps be the personal pro-
noun?
But what runs across it? Four-letter word meaning something
With a bias towards its opposite, the second letter
Must be the same as the one-letter word.
       It is time
We left these puzzles and started to be ourselves
And started to live, is it not?

Louis Macneice

THE CLIMBERS

To the cold peak without their careful women
(Who watching children climbing into dreams
Go dispossessed at home). The mountain moves
Away at every climb and steps are hard
Frozen along the glacier. Every man
Tied to the rope constructs himself alone.

And not the summit reached nor any pole
Touched is the wished embrace, but still to move
And as the mountain climbs to see it whole
And each mind's landscape growing more complete
As sinews strain and all the muscles knot.

One at the peak is small. His disappointment
The coloured flag flown at the lonely top,
And all the valley's motive grown obscure.
He envies the large toilers halfway there
Who still possess the mountain by desire
And, not arriving, dream in no resentment.

Elizabeth Jennings

THE SUMMIT

(*from* Everest Climbed)

The sun went down, from peak to peak
The long purple shadows creeping.
Tired and weak,
They yawned and settled down to sleeping—
Hillary bunched in his narrow place,
Tenzing stretched on the brink of space.
While the rude wind roared them a lullaby
To a tearing tune,
Hillary, sleepless, braced for each blast,
Clung to the walls and anchored them fast
And none too soon,
Till the wind sank down and the silent sky
Was lit with the stars and the moon.

At four in the morning he woke. His feet
And legs were numb to the knees and freezing.
But the peaks were aglow in the early light
And the frost was easing.
His boots were white and stiff from the weather,
So he cooked them over the primus flame
till up to his nostrils fiercely came
The stench of burning leather.
When they'd carefully checked the oxygen gauges
And fixed their boots and loaded backs,
Away they stepped in easy stages,
Each in turn kicking the tracks.

They toiled to the foot of the Southern Peak
Where the slope was steep with snow half-stuck—
And slippery, treacherous indeed
When Hillary's turn it was to lead.
The first step firm, the second crumbled,
And down in a shower of white he tumbled.
Tenzing was ready—on the lightning slope
He halted him with axe and rope.
Thus once before in the Icefall snow
The Tiger had held him, bruised and numb,
On the icy brink of Kingdom Come
Whose chasm yawned below.

Undaunted still, with desperate skill,
Cautious as blind men crossing a street
They crept four hundred faltering feet.
And they'd reached and passed the Southern Peak
When Hillary's rope began to drag
And Tenzing staggered and fell in his track,
Tottered and swayed and gasped for breath.
The face in the icicle-crusted mask
Was pale as death.
But Hillary found where the strength was going—
The oxygen tube was jammed with ice.
With his glove he knocked it free—in a trice
The life was flowing.

Their steps were weary, keen was the wind,
Fast vanishing their oxygen fuel,
And the summit ridge was fanged and cruel—
Fanged and cruel, bitter and bare.

And now with a sickening shock
They saw before them a towering wall
Of smooth and holdless rock.
O ghastly fear—with the goal so near
To find the way was blocked!
On one side darkly the mountain dropped,
On the other two plunging miles of peak
Shot from the dizzy skyline down
In a silver streak.

'No hope of turning the bluff to the west,'
Said Hillary. 'What's that I see to the east?
A worm-wide crack between cornice and rock—
Will it hold? I can try it at least.'
He called to Tenzing, 'Draw in the slack!'
Then levered himself right into the crack
And, kicking his spikes in the frozen crust,
Wriggled up with his back,
With arms and feet and shoulders he fought,
Inch by sweating inch, then caught
At the crest and grabbed for the light of day.
There was time, as he struggled for breath, to pray
For all the might that a man could wish—
Then he heaved at the rope till over the lip
Brave Tenzing, hauled from the deep, fell flop
Like a monstrous gaping fish.

Was the summit theirs?—they puffed and panted—
No, for the ridge still upward pointed.
On they plodded, Martian-weird
With pouting mask and icicle beard
That cracked and tinkled, broke and rattled,
As on with pounding hearts they battled,
On to the summit—
Till at last the ridge began to drop.
Two swings, two whacks of Hillary's axe,
And they stood on top.

Ian Serraillier

Urban and Rural Lanscapes

ENTERING THE CITY

The city lies ahead. The vale
is cluttering as the train speeds through.
Hacked woods fall back; the scoop and swell
of cooling towers swing into view.

Acres of clinker, slag-heaps, roads
where lorries rev and tip all night,
railway sidings, broken sheds,
brutally bare in arc-light,

summon me to a present far
from Pericles's Athens, Caesar's Rome,
to follow again the river's scar
squirming beneath detergent foam.

I close the book and rub the glass;
a glance ambiguously dark
entertains briefly scrap-yards, rows
of houses, and a treeless park,

like passing thoughts. Across my head
sundry familiar and strange
denizens of the city tread
vistas I would, and would not, change.

Birth-place and home! The diesel's whine
flattens. Excited and defiled
once more, I heave the window down
and thrust my head out like a child.

Tony Connor

LOVERS IN CLOWES PARK

The Hall decayed, and then came down;
the corporation bought the parkland:
tree and wall, lake without a bottom
and fabled pike within it, grown

large as a man. We are late
upon the scene; the nursery garden—
rose and chrysanthemum growing over
the great family's abandoned site—

itself's abandoned. The giant fish
is quite discredited since the waterworks
dredged and restocked the weed-grown shallows
whose depth is known to the inch. That flash

of late sunlight is off the glazed
bricks of the 'Ladies', nestled in privets,
and by the soggy path a bulldozer
dozes amidst the earth it's raised

to lay new drains. The evening sky
disgorges chemicals in silence;
leaves and grasses bend, ever so little,
under each new moment's weight. My eye,

encountering yours, takes comfort from
the falling soot between, the public
neatness of squalor. Not unworthy,
as last we have come home to our true kingdom.

Tony Connor

EDINBURGH COURTYARD IN JULY

Hot light is smeared as thick as paint
On these ramshackle tenements. Stones smell
Of dust. Their hoisting into quaint
Crowsteps, corbels, carved with fool and saint,
Hold fathoms of heat, like water in a well.

Cliff-dwellers have poked out from their
High cave-mouths brilliant rags on drying-lines;
They hang still, dazzling in the glare,
And lead the eye up, ledge by ledge, to where
A chimney's tilted helmet winks and shines.

And water from a broken drain
Splashes a glassy hand out in the air
That breaks in an unbraiding rain
And falls still fraying, to become a stain
That spreads by footsteps, ghosting everywhere.

Norman MacCaig

NOVEMBER NIGHT, EDINBURGH

The night tinkles like ice in glasses.
Leaves are glued to the pavement with frost.
The brown air fumes at the shop windows,
Tries the doors, and sidles past.

I gulp down winter raw. The heady
Darkness swirls with tenements.
In a brown fuzz of cottonwool
Lamps fade up crags, die into pits.

Frost in my lungs is harsh as leaves
Scraped up on paths.—I look up, there,
A high roof sails, at the mast-head
Fluttering a grey and ragged star.

The world's a bear shrugged in his den.
It's snug and close in the snoring night.
And outside like chrysanthemums
The fog unfolds its bitter scent.

Norman MacCaig

The fat flakes fall
In parachute invasion from the yellow sky.
The streets are quiet and surprised; the snow
Clutters the roofs with a wet crust, but not
Dry harbour is found on soil or wall.

In the town
The fledgling sparrows are puzzled and take fright;
The weedy hair of the slagbank in an hour turns white.
Flakes fill the tulips in backyard plots;
The chimneys snow upward and the snow smokes down.

Beyond the fells
Dawn lumbers up, and the peaks are white through the mist.
The young bracken is buttoned with snow; the knobs
Of crabapple trees are in bloom again, and blobs
Hang on the nettles like canterbury bells.

The job is mine
And everyone's: to force our blood into the bitter day.
The hawthorn scorched and blasted by the flames of the wind
On the sheltered side greens out a dogged spray—
And this is our example, our duty and our sign.

Norman Nicholson

ON THE CLOSING OF MILLOM IRONWORKS: SEPTEMBER 1968

Wandering by the heave of the town park, wondering
Which way the day will drift,
On the spur of a habit I turn to the feathered
Weathercock of the furnace chimneys.
                            But no grey smoke-tail
Pointers the mood of the wind. The hum
And blare that for a hundred years
Drummed at the town's deaf ears
Now fills the air with the roar of its silence.
They'll need no more to swill the slag-dust off the
    windows;
The curtains will be cleaner
And the grass plots greener

92

Round the Old Folks' council flats. The tanged autumnal
    mist
Is filtered free of soot and sulphur,
And the wind blows in untainted.
It's beautiful to breathe the sharp night air.
And, look, scrawled on the walls of the Working Men's:
'No-one starves in the Welfare State.'
                                    They stand
By the churchyard gate,
Hands in pockets, shoulders to the slag,
The men whose fathers stood there back in '28,
When their sons were at school with me.
                                    The town
Rolls round the century's bleak orbit.
                                    Down
On the ebb-tide sands, the five-funnelled
Battleship of the furnaces lies beached and rusting;
Run aground, not foundered;
Not a crack in her hull;
Lacking but a loan to float her off.
                                    The Market
Square is busy as the men file by
To sign on at the 'Brew'. But not a face
Tilts upward, no-one enquires of the sky.
The smoke prognosticates no how
Or why of any practical tomorrow.
For what does it matter if it rains all day?
And what's the good of knowing
Which way the wind is blowing
When whichever way it blows it's a cold wind now?

Norman Nicholson

A VISIT TO BRONTËLAND

The road climbs from the valley past the public
Park and turns, at the Haworth Co-operative Stores,
Into the grey stone village, and the steep
Street leading to the Parsonage, the Inn, the W.C.s;
To the Church of St Michael and All Angels, high in trees.

The West Lane Baptists are putting on
Patience, the playbills say. The Heathcliffe Tearooms are aglow

With English teachers in sensible tweeds. Bearded cyclists
Lean on their pedals, and their saddles shine and sway
Up the hill to the Y.H.A.

Across the valley thick with mills
The fellside rises like an aerial map
Of fields and drystone walls and farms.
Pylons saunter over with a minimum of fuss,
And round the bend from Keighley comes the Brontë bus.

An arty signboard poses Charlotte in a crinoline
And ringlets, penning *Jane Eyre*, at a table, with a quill.
'This must be *it*'.—The wondering Americans, like Technicolor
    ads.,
Have reverence plainly written on their open faces.
They know just how one should behave in hallowed places.

A sea of scriptured slabs
Shines in the graveyard under the twilight rain.
The cold winds are crying in the trees.
New heights above the pines
Are wuthered by tractors of open-cast mines.

The church where the Brontës worshipped
Is long demolished. Only a brass plate
Marks where their bones are buried. Smothered
In Parks Committee geraniums, Anne lies alone
In Scarborough Old Churchyard, under a dolled-up stone.

Now, in the village roofs, the television aerial aspires.
No idle toy would have tempted Branwell
From the Bull, and brandy; or kept that sister
From her tragic poems. They knew they had nothing but the moor
And themselves. It is we, who want all, who are poor.

James Kirkup

LEEDS 2

Houses once grand now condemned,
Gardens decayed to a playground
For ragged children, trees dirty
    To touch are lit every morning

By the indirect sun; mist gathers
Here disclosing only green and brightness
And the everywhere elegant lines
Of trees and rooftops against the air.
Rubbish on grass doesn't offend
Then, nor could I wish for any other
Environment, nor anything lovelier
Than five minutes of standing
In the bare hall where door ajar
And grimed fanlight frame the garden;
Reversing the Dutch painter's view
Also in my house-pride being perverse.
At mid-day lying on the grass
The hard ground and dung smells
And flung away bottles constrict
The place to a poor bit of nature,
Only better than a concrete yard;
But evening or snow, or rain
Adds the glow of emotion, sets off
Vague notions of regret for this
Victim of time the coming people
Will clear away. This old square
Is dying late. The people who lived
Here by choice have all left,
And through what used to be a gate
Come students, labourers and refugees
For temporary shelter from the traffic,
Audible all night like threatening seas
Beyond the private garden and the trees.

James Simmons

HOUSING SCHEME

All summer through
The field drank showers of larksong;
Offering in return
The hospitality of grasses,
And flowers kneedeep.

Over those wide acres
Trooped the plovers,
Mourning and lamenting as evening fell.

95

From the deep hedgerows
Where the foam of meadowsweet broke,
The rabbits and mice
Peeped out, and boldly sat in the sun.

But when the oaks were bronzing,
Steamrollers and brickcarts
Broke through the hedges.
The white-haired grasses, and the seedpods
Disappeared into the mud,
And the larks were silent, the plovers gone.

Then over the newlaid roads
And the open trenches of drains,
Rose a hoarding to face the highway,
'Build your house in the country.'

Richard Church

HERE

Swerving east, from rich industrial shadows
And traffic all night north; swerving through fields
Too thin and thistled to be called meadows,
And now and then a harsh-named halt, that shields
Workmen at dawn; swerving to solitude
Of skies and scarecrows, haystacks, hares and pheasants,
And the widening river's slow presence,
The piled gold clouds, the shining gull-marked mud,

Gathers to the surprise of a large town:
Here domes and statues, spires and cranes cluster
Beside grain-scattered streets, barge-crowded water,
And residents from raw estates, brought down
The dead straight miles by stealing flat-faced trolleys,
Push through plate-glass swing doors to their desires—
Cheap suits, red kitchen-ware, sharp shoes, iced lollies,
Electric mixers, toasters, washers, driers—

A cut-price crowd, urban yet simple, dwelling
Where only salesmen and relations come
Within a terminate and fishy-smelling
Pastoral of ships up streets, the slave museum,

Tattoo-shops, consulates, grim head-scarfed wives;
And out beyond its mortgaged half-built edges
Fast-shadowed wheat-fields, running high as hedges,
Isolate villages, where removed lives

Loneliness clarifies. Here silence stands
Like heat. Here leaves unnoticed thicken,
Hidden weeds flower, neglected waters quicken,
Luminously-peopled air ascends;
And past the poppies bluish neutral distance
Ends the land suddenly beyond a beach
Of shapes and shingle. Here is unfenced existence:
Facing the sun, untalkative, out of reach.

Philip Larkin

THE VIEW FROM THE WINDOW

Like a painting it is set before one,
But less brittle, ageless; these colours
Are renewed daily with variations
Of light and distance that no painter
Achieves or suggests. Then there is movement,
Change, as slowly the cloud bruises
Are healed by sunlight, or snow caps
A black mood; but gold at evening
To cheer the heart. All through history
The great brush has not rested,
Nor the paint dried; yet what eye,
Looking coolly, or, as we now,
Through the tears' lenses, ever saw
This work and it was not finished.

R. S. Thomas

THE BULB FIELD

Up on top of the cliff there, that
Green patch, lighter, more domestic
Looking than the brackeny wastes
Around it, that's a farmer's field.
It sits right over the sea, swell
Slapping rocks all summer, hear it?

And as for winter, you can guess
The splintering force of the white
Dragons roaring against the land,
The exploding sea heard for miles,
Fountaining spray clear of the high
Cliffs even, wetting the shoulders
Of the workmen hunched against it.

I've known men faint in that field, cold
Killing their fingers, blasting wind
Sucking the breath right out of them.
That wind can blow tractors over.
It's an odd field to work in, too.
You jump, seeing the ground stop short,
A gull's back swinging a hundred
Feet below you. Space is a fright.

You should see that spot in spring, though,
Thick and yellow with bulbs blooming
For market. Most people like them.
They wag bright heads, put fragrance on
Someone's table, look delicate,
And bring good prices. Picking them
Cripples backs, and while the season
Lasts, bunching and boxing take till
Past midnight. Fingers even bleed.

A troubled cliff: you'd never think,
For all the struggle, much would grow
In a place like that. But most years
It has its useful spell, if work
And weather can come to terms, force
Blunt shoots from the bulbs, and pattern
The spring ground with those brilliant
Dancers. Eyes are pleased and wallets
Thickened. The cliff has meaning then;
It shines with, and is stripped of, gold.

John Cassidy

THE PRESERVATION OF LANDSCAPES

Again summer journeys across England
take me past landscapes become familiar
with five years' travelling. The country comes
alive again with its beeches and elms,
composing its prettiness in my mind
with a fleeting abstraction of colour.

Gliders, pinned to the sky above Cambridge,
are still as eagles for a moment, then
are swift as the homeward flight of swallows.
I drive across the flat Cambridgeshire farms
and find the sun absorbed in a lonely
colloquy with the land, bargaining growth.

The train does ninety on the run between
Leicester and Derby, leaps across the Trent,
and, as a plane overshoots a runway,
briefly avoids industrial Midlands
to nibble through pastureland, devouring
the coarse grass with the quickness of locusts.

Dark pine-forests on the road to Portsmouth;
aspens, whose leaves catch the breeze and the light
as do sequins on a hat at Ascot,
and the gay ash-trees on the road to Bath;
and the fields, the fields are like coloured bits
of paper pasting England on my mind.

I share the anxiety of Englishmen
about England, prizing each field, each tree,
each tuft of grass above the incursions
of concrete and steel. O, sad, sad, England!
The beeches in East Riding, too, among the moors,
are yellow with the dust from upturned roads.

And yet I would rather have steel, rather
go giddy on winding car-park buildings
than look at the fiercely sunlit landscapes
of Southeast Asia where foreign jets
have cut the jungle for airstrips and the earth
is cleaved at the centre, deflowered with bombs.

Zulfikar Ghose

WOODS AND KESTREL

The quiet woods in the hot Eastertide
Sleep to the dancing chime of village bells,
Under the scarp of the tall down that swells
To a steep shouldered crest on the north side.

The gas thin film of green leaves, wreathing smoke
In the black trees, sap swelling in the heat:
Wet empty axe-cropped clearing at their feet
Where moss-banked primroses in the sun soak.

Deep from the hill the opened floor appears,
White scattered chips and face ridged boles
Of the felled trees; stacked ash and hazel poles,
Where they have cut the copse, as each ten years.

A kestrel, umber mantle and black wings,
From the bare down, out of the empty skies,
Deep into the wooded hollow, kite-winged, flies,
And in curved line, down through the tree-tops, swings.

Thence comes the steel flash of an axe's head,
Stooping in hawk-swift curve of metal bright
On soft wood, the sap-moist chips spurting white.
Up the slow hill the ringing bell thuds spread.

With sunshine in brown eyes, on rippling breast,
The kestrel up and away from the axe stroke lifts,
And swirling up the blue weald landscape shifts
To the forest ridge's pine-wood darkened crest.

Julian Bell

WILTSHIRE DOWNS

The cuckoo's double note
Loosened like bubbles from a drowning throat
Floats through the air
In mockery of pipit, lark and stare.

The stable-boys thud by
Their horses slinging divots at the sky

And with bright hooves
Printing the sodden turf with lucky grooves.

As still as a windhover
A shepherd in his flapping coat leans over
His tall sheep-crook
And shearlings, tegs and yoes cons like a book.

And one tree-crowned long barrow
Stretched like a sow that has brought forth her farrow
Hides a king's bones
Lying like broken sticks among the stones.

Andrew Young

CORNISH CLIFFS

Those moments, tasted once and never done,
Of long surf breaking in the mid-day sun,
A far-off blow-hole booming like a gun—

The seagulls plane and circle out of sight
Below this thirsty, thrift-encrusted height,
The veined sea-campion buds burst into white

And gorse turns tawny orange, seen beside
Pale drifts of primroses cascading wide
To where the slate falls sheer into the tide.

More than in gardened Surrey, nature spills
A wealth of heather, kidney-vetch and squills
Over these long-defended Cornish hills.

A gun-emplacement of the latest war
Looks older than the hill fort built before
Saxon or Norman headed for the shore.

And in the shadowless, unclouded glare
Deep blue above us fades to whiteness where
A misty sea-line meets the wash of air.

Nut-smell of gorse and honey-smell of ling
Waft out to sea the freshness of the spring
On sunny shallows, green and whispering.

The wideness which the lark-song gives the sky
Shrinks at the clang of sea-birds sailing by
Whose notes are tuned to days when seas are high.

From today's calm, the lane's enclosing green
Leads inland to a usual Cornish scene—
Slate cottages with sycamore between,

Small fields and tellymasts and wires and poles
With, as the everlasting ocean rolls,
Two chapels built for half a hundred souls.

John Betjeman

Wars and Rumours of Wars

SPRING OFFENSIVE

Halted against the shade of a last hill,
They fed, and lying easy, were at ease
And, finding comfortable chests and knees,
Carelessly slept. But many there stood still
To face the stark, blank sky beyond the ridge,
Knowing their feet had come to the end of the world.

Marvelling they stood, and watched the long grass swirled
By the May breeze, murmurous with wasp and midge,
For though the summer oozed into their veins
Like an injected drug for their bodies' pains,
Sharp on their souls hung the imminent line of grass,
Fearfully flashed the sky's mysterious glass.

Hour after hour they ponder the warm field—
And the far valley behind, where the buttercup
Had blessed with gold their slow boots coming up,
Where even the little brambles would not yield,
But clutched and clung to them like sorrowing hands;
They breathe like trees unstirred.

Till like a cold gust thrills the little word
At which each body and its soul begird
And tighten them for battle. No alarms
Of bugles, no high flags, no clamorous haste—
Only a lift and flare of eyes that faced
The sun, like a friend with whom their love is done.
O larger shone that smile against the sun—
Mightier than His whose bounty these have spurned.

So, soon they topped the hill, and raced together
Over an open stretch of herb and heather
Exposed. And instantly the whole sky burned

With fury against them; earth set sudden cups
In thousands for their blood; and the green slope
Chasmed and steepened sheer to infinite space.

*   *   *

Of them who running on that last high place
Leapt to swift unseen bullets, or went up
On the hot blast and fury of hell's upsurge,
Or plunged and fell away past this world's verge,
Some say God caught them even before they fell.

But what say such as from existence' brink
Ventured but drave too swift to sink,
The few who rushed in the body to enter hell,
And there out-fiending all its fiends and flames
With superhuman inhumanities,
Long-famous glories, immemorial shames—
And crawling slowly back, have by degrees
Regained cool peaceful air in wonder—
Why speak not they of comrades that went under?

Wilfred Owen

DULCE ET DECORUM EST

Bent double, like old beggars under sacks,
Knock-kneed, coughing like hags, we cursed through sludge,
Till on the haunting flares we turned our backs
And towards our distant rest began to trudge.
Men marched asleep. Many had lost their boots,
But limped on, blood-shod. All went lame; all blind;
Drunk with fatigue; deaf even to the hoots
Of tired, outstripped Five-Nines that dropped behind.

Gas! Gas! Quick, boys!—An ecstasy of fumbling,
Fitting the clumsy helmets just in time;
But someone still was yelling out and stumbling
And flound'ring like a man in fire or lime . . .
Dim, through the misty panes and thick green light,
As under a green sea, I saw him drowning.

In all my dreams, before my helpless sight,
He plunges at me, guttering, choking, drowning.

If in some smothering dreams you too could pace
Behind the wagon that we flung him in,
And watch the white eyes writhing in his face,
His hanging face, like a devil's sick of sin;
If you could hear, at every jolt, the blood
Come gargling from the froth-corrupted lungs,
Obscene as cancer, bitter as the cud
Of vile, incurable sores on innocent tongues,—
My friend, you would not tell with such high zest
To children ardent for some desperate glory,
The old Lie: *Dulce et decorum est*
Pro patria mori.

Wilfred Owen

THE SENTRY

We'd found an old Boche dug-out, and he knew,
And gave us hell, for shell on frantic shell
Hammered on top, but never quite burst through.
Rain, guttering down in waterfalls of slime,
Kept slush waist-high and rising hour by hour,
And choked the steps too thick with clay to climb.
What murk of air remained stank old, and sour
With fumes of whizz-bangs, and the smell of men
Who'd lived there years, and left their curse in the den,
If not their corpses . . .
                                        There we herded from the blast
Of whizz-bangs, but one found our door at last,—
Buffeting eyes and breath, snuffing the candles,
And thud! flump! thud! down the steep steps came thumping
And sploshing the flood, deluging muck—
The sentry's body; then, his rifle, handles
Of old Boche bombs, and mud in ruck on ruck.
We dredged him up, for killed, until he whined
'O sir, my eyes—I'm blind—I'm blind, I'm blind!'
Coaxing, I held a flame against his lids
And he said if he could see the least blurred light
He was not blind; in time he'd get all right.
'I can't,' he sobbed. Eyeballs, huge-bulged like squids',
Watch my dreams still; but I forgot him there
In posting next for duty, and sending a scout
To beg a stretcher somewhere, and flound'ring about
To other posts under the shrieking air.

Those other wretches, how they bled and spewed,
And one who would have drowned himself for good,—
I try not to remember these things now.
Let dread hark back for one word only: how
Half listening to that sentry's moans and jumps,
And the wild chattering of his broken teeth,
Renewed most horribly whenever crumps
Pummelled the roof and slogged the air beneath—
Through the dense din, I say, we heard him shout
'I see your light!' But ours had long died out.

Wilfred Owen

STRANGE MEETING

It seemed that out of battle I escaped
Down some profound dull tunnel, long since scooped
Through granites which titanic wars had groined.
Yet also there encumbered sleepers groaned,
Too fast in thought or death to be bestirred.
Then, as I probed them, one sprang up, and stared
With piteous recognition in fixed eyes,
Lifting distressful hands as if to bless.
And by his smile, I knew that sullen hall,
By his dead smile I knew we stood in Hell.
With a thousand pains that vision's face was grained;
Yet no blood reached there from the upper ground,
And no guns thumped, or down the flues made moan.
'Strange friend,' I said, 'here is no cause to mourn.'
'None,' said that other, 'save the undone years,
The hopelessness. Whatever hope is yours,
Was my life also; I went hunting wild
After the wildest beauty in the world,
Which lies not calm in eyes, or braided hair,
But mocks the steady running of the hour,
And if it grieves, grieves richlier than here.
For of my glee might many men have laughed,
And of my weeping something had been left,
Which must die now. I mean the truth untold,
The pity of war, the pity war distilled.
Now men will go content with what we spoiled,
Or, discontent, boil bloody, and be spilled.
They will be swift with swiftness of the tigress.

None will break ranks, though nations trek from progress.
Courage was mine, and I had mystery,
Wisdom was mine, and I had mastery;
To miss the march of this retreating world
Into vain citadels that are not walled.
Then, when much blood had clogged their chariot-wheels,
I would go up and wash them from sweet wells,
Even with truths that lie too deep for taint.
I would have poured my spirit without stint
But not through wounds; not on the cess of war.
Foreheads of men have bled where no wounds were.
I am the enemy you killed, my friend.
I knew you in this dark: for so you frowned
Yesterday through me as you jabbed and killed.
I parried; but my hands were loath and cold.
Let us sleep now . . .'

Wilfred Owen

MEMORIAL TABLET

(War of 1914-18)

Squire nagged and bullied till I went to fight
(Under Lord Derby's scheme). I died in hell—
(They called it Passchendaele); my wound was slight,
And I was hobbling back, and then a shell
Burst slick upon the duck-boards; so I fell
Into the bottomless mud, and lost the light.

In sermon-time, while Squire is in his pew,
He gives my gilded name a thoughtful stare;
For though low down upon the list, I'm there:
'In proud and glorious memory'—that's my due.
Two bleeding years I fought in France for Squire;
I suffered anguish that he's never guessed;
Once I came home on leave; and then went west.
What greater glory could a man desire?

Siegfried Sassoon

The wooden cabinet of the television
is their coffin; they are
trapped behind the screen
like so many ants in a jam jar.
Hundreds of soldiers swarming
out of endless trenches:
dots on the muddy terrain,
blurs through the smoke,
silhouettes against the skyline,
jerking puppets re-enacting
the same celluloid charge
for the past fifty-five years.
The film is interspersed a dozen times
by different French statesmen,
each posing briefly
by the open door of a limousine.
The battle is also abandoned at intervals
in favour of generals shaking hands
(always with a glance towards the camera)
queues of women in wide-brimmed hats,
and once, unforgettably,
a scene from the eastern front:
snow-covered corpses in the foreground
and a tiny horse and cart
just visible, far away in the distance,
moving slowly on the white road
like a sluggish blowfly
on the margin of a newspaper.
There are also the huge recoiling cannons
and the quaintly soundless explosions:
monotonously identical, irrespective
of whose shells caused them
or of whose mud they scattered.
Just when things are looking grim
—the Germans have got those smart, new helmets
and have mounted a counter-offensive—
the Kaiser abdicates,
the German navy mutinies at Kiel,
the Americans are strengthening the allied lines,
and the Great War ends.
It is the scale of such carnage
which is hardest to grasp;

we have seen four years
compressed into an hour and a half
and our sense of perspective is shell-shocked.
When we turn off the television
we are almost tempted
to kneel on the floor and search
for any small, dead or wounded soldiers
that might have fallen out.

Allan Burgis

ULTIMA RATIO REGUM

(The Final Argument of Rulers)

The guns spell money's ultimate reason
In letters of lead on the spring hillside.
But the boy lying dead under the olive trees
Was too young and too silly
To have been notable to their important eye.
He was a better target for a kiss.

When he lived, tall factory hooters never summoned him.
Nor did restaurant plate-glass doors revolve to wave him in.
His name never appeared in the papers.
The world maintained its traditional wall
Round the dead with their gold sunk deep as a well,
Whilst his life, intangible as a Stock Exchange rumour, drifted
    outside.

O too lightly he threw down his cap
One day when the breeze threw petals from the trees.
The unflowering wall sprouted with guns,
Machine-gun anger quickly scythed the grasses;
Flags and leaves fell from hands and branches;
The tweed cap rotted in the nettles.

Consider his life which was valueless
In terms of employment, hotel ledgers, news files.
Consider. One bullet in ten thousand kills a man.
Ask. Was so much expenditure justified
On the death of one so young and so silly
Lying under the olive trees, O world, O death?

Stephen Spender

Conferences, adjournments, ultimatums
    Flights in the air, castles in the air,
The autopsy of treaties, dynamite under the bridges,
    The end of *laissez-faire*.
After the warm days the rain comes pimpling
    The paving stones with white
And with the rain the national conscience, creeping,
    Seeping through the night.
And in the sodden park on Sunday protest
    Meetings assemble not, as so often, now
Merely to advertise some patent panacea
    But simply to avow
The need to hold the ditch; a bare avowal
    That may perhaps imply
Death at the doors in a week but perhaps in the long run
    Exposure of the lie.
Think of a number, double it, treble it, square it,
    And sponge it out
And repeat *ad lib.* and mark the slate with crosses;
    There is no time to doubt
If the puzzle really has an answer. Hitler yells on the wireless,
    The night is damp and still
And I hear dull blows on wood outside my window;
    They are cutting down the trees on Primrose Hill.
The wood is white like the roast flesh of chicken,
    Each tree falling like a closing fan;
No more looking at the view from seats beneath the branches,
    Everything is going to plan;
They want the crest of this hill for anti-aircraft,
    The guns will take the view
And searchlights probe the heavens for bacilli
    With narrow wands of blue.
And the rain came on as I watched the territorials
    Sawing and chopping and pulling on ropes like a team
In a village tug-of-war; and I found my dog had vanished
    And thought 'This is the end of the old regime,'
But found the police had got her at St John's Wood station
    And fetched her in the rain and went for a cup
Of coffee to an all-night shelter and heard a taxi-driver
    Say 'It turns me up
When I see these soldiers in lorries'—rumble of tumbrils
    Drums in the trees

Breaking the eardrums of the ravished dryads—
   It turns me up; a coffee, please.
And as I go out I see a windscreen-wiper
   In an empty car
Wiping away like mad and I feel astounded
   That things have gone so far.

Louis Macneice

EMBASSY

As evening fell the day's oppression lifted;
Tall peaks came into focus; it had rained:
Across wide lawns and cultured flowers drifted
The conversation of the highly trained.

Thin gardeners watched them pass and priced their shoes:
A chauffeur waited, reading in the drive,
For them to finish their exchange of views;
It looked a picture of the way to live.

Far off, no matter what good they intended,
The armies waited for a verbal error
With well-made instruments for causing pain,

And on the issue of their charm depended
A land laid waste with all its young men slain,
Its women weeping, and its towns in terror.

W. H. Auden

UNSEEN FIRE

This is a damned inhuman sort of war.
I have been fighting in a dressing-gown
Most of the night; I cannot see the guns,
The sweating gun-detachments or the planes;

I swear down here before a symbol thrown
Upon a screen, sift facts, initiate
Swift calculations and swift orders; wait
For the precise split-second to order fire.

111

We chant our ritual words; beyond the phones
A ghost repeats the orders to the guns:
One Fire . . . Two Fire . . . ghosts answer:
               the guns roar
Abruptly; and an aircraft waging war
Inhumanly from nearly five miles height
Meets our bouquet of death—and turns sharp right.

*   *   *

This is a damned unnatural sort of war;
The pilot sits among the clouds, quite sure
About the values he is fighting for;
He cannot hear beyond his veil of sound,

He cannot see the people on the ground;
He only knows that on the sloping map
Of sea-fringed town and country people creep
Like ants—and who cares if ants laugh or weep?

To us he is no more than a machine
Shown on an instrument: what can he mean
In human terms?—a man, somebody's son,
Proud of his skill; compact of flesh and bone
Fragile as Icarus—and our desire
To see that damned machine come down on fire.

R. N. Currey

THE EVACUEE

She woke up under a loose quilt
Of leaf patterns, woven by the light
At the small window, busy with the boughs
Of a young cherry; but wearily she lay,
Waiting for the siren, slow to trust
Nature's deceptive peace, and then afraid
Of the long silence, she would have crept
Uneasily from the bedroom with its frieze
Of fresh sunlight, had not a cock crowed,
Shattering the surface of that limpid pool
Of stillness, and before the ripples died
One by one in the field's shallows,
The farm woke with uninhibited din.

And now the noise and not the silence drew her
Down the bare stairs at great speed.
The sounds and voices were a rough sheet
Waiting to catch her, as though she leaped
From a scorched storey of the charred past.

And there the table and the gallery
Of farm faces trying to be kind
Beckoned her nearer, and she sat down
Under an awning of salt hams.

And so she grew, a small bird in the nest
Of welcome that was built about her,
Home now after so long away
In the flowerless streets of the drab town.
The men watched her busy with the hens,
The soft flesh ripening warm as corn
On the sticks of limbs, the grey eyes clear,
Rinsed with dew of their long dread.
The men watched her, and, nodding, smiled
With earth's charity, patient and strong.

R. S. Thomas

WATCHING POST

A hill flank overlooking the Axe valley.
Among the stubble a farmer and I keep watch
For whatever may come to injure our countryside—
Light-signals, parachutes, bombs, or sea-invaders.
The moon looks over the hill's shoulder, and hope
Mans the old ramparts of an English night.

In a house down there was Marlborough born. One night
Monmouth marched to his ruin out of that valley.
Beneath our castled hill, where Britons kept watch,
Is a church where the Drakes, old lords of this countryside,
Sleep under their painted effigies. No invaders
Can dispute their legacy of toughness and hope.

Two counties away, over Bristol, the searchlights hope
To find what danger is in the air tonight.
Presently gunfire from Portland reaches our valley

Tapping like an ill-hung door in a draught. My watch
Says nearly twelve. All over the countryside
Moon-dazzled men are peering out for invaders.

The farmer and I talk for a while of invaders:
But soon we turn to crops—the annual hope,
Making of cider, prizes for ewes. Tonight
How many hearts along this war-mazed valley
Dream of a day when at peace they may work and watch
The small sufficient wonders of the countryside.

Image or fact, we both in the countryside
Have found our natural law, and until invaders
Come will answer its need: for both of us, hope
Means a harvest from small beginnings, who this night
While the moon sorts out into shadow and shape our valley,
A farmer and a poet, are keeping watch.

C. Day Lewis

NAMING OF PARTS

Today we have naming of parts. Yesterday,
We had daily cleaning. And tomorrow morning,
We shall have what to do after firing. But today,
Today we have naming of parts. Japonica
Glistens like coral in all of the neighbouring gardens,
        And today we have naming of parts.

This is the lower sling swivel. And this
Is the upper sling swivel, whose use you will see,
When you are given your slings. And this is the piling swivel,
Which in your case you have not got. The branches
Hold in the gardens their silent, eloquent gestures,
        Which in our case we have not got.

This is the safety-catch, which is always released
With an easy flick of the thumb. And please do not let me
See anyone using his finger. You can do it quite easy
If you have any strength in your thumb. The blossoms
Are fragile and motionless, never letting anyone see
        Any of them using their finger.

And this you can see is the bolt. The purpose of this
Is to open the breech, as you see. We can slide it
Rapidly backwards and forwards: we call this
Easing the spring. And rapidly backwards and forwards
The early bees are assaulting and fumbling the flowers:
    They call it easing the Spring.

They call it easing the spring: it is perfectly easy
If you have any strength in your thumb: like the bolt,
And the breech, and the cocking-piece, and the point of balance,
Which in our case we have not got; and the almond-blossom
Silent in all of the gardens and the bees going backwards and
    forwards,
    For today we have naming of parts.

Henry Reed

VERGISSMEINNICHT (Forget-me-not)

Three weeks gone and the combatants gone,
returning over the nightmare ground
we found the place again, and found
the soldier sprawling in the sun.

The frowning barrel of his gun
overshadowing. As we came on
that day, he hit my tank with one
like the entry of a demon.

Look. Here in the gunpit spoil
the dishonoured picture of his girl
who has put: *Steffi. Vergissmeinnicht*
in a copybook gothic script.

We see him almost with content,
abased, and seeming to have paid
and mocked at by his own equipment
that's hard and good when he's decayed.

But she would weep to see today
how on his skin the swart flies move;
the dust upon the paper eye
and the burst stomach like a cave.

For here the lover and killer are mingled
who had one body and one heart.
And death who had the soldier singled
has done the lover mortal hurt.

Tunisia (May-June) 1943

Keith Douglas

THE MONUMENTS OF HIROSHIMA

The roughly estimated ones, who do not sort well
    with our common phrases,
Who are by no means eating roots of dandelion,
    or pushing up the daisies,

The more or less anonymous, to whom no human idiom
    can apply,
Who neither passed away, or on,
    nor went before, nor vanished on a sigh.

Little of peace for them to rest in, less of them
    to rest in peace:
Dust to dust a swift transition, ashes to ash
    with awful ease.

Their only monument will be of others' casting—
A Tower of Peace, a Hall of Peace, a Bridge of Peace—
    who might have wished for something lasting,
Like a wooden box.

D. J. Enright

FOREIGN AFFAIRS

We are two countries girded for the war,
Whisking our scouts across the pricked frontier
To ravage in each other's fields, cut lines
Along the lacework of strategic nerves,
Loot stores; while here and there,
In ambushes that trace a valley's curves,
Stark witness to the dangerous charge we bear,
A house ignites, a train's derailed, a bridge
Blows up sky-high, and water floods the mines.

Who first attacked? Who turned the other cheek?
Aggression perpetrated is as soon
Denied, and insult rubbed into the injury
By cunning agents trained in these affairs,
With whom it's touch-and-go, don't-tread-on-me,
I-dare-you-to, keep-off, and kiss-my-hand.
Tempers could sharpen knives, and do; we live
In states provocative
Where frowning headlines scare the coffee cream
And doomsday is the eighth day of the week.

Our exit through the slammed and final door
Is twenty times rehearsed, but when we face
The imminence of cataclysmic rupture,
A lesser pride goes down upon its knees.
Two countries separated by desire!—
Whose diplomats speed back and forth by plane,
Portmanteaus stuffed with fresh apologies
Outdated by events before they land.
Negotiations wear them out: they're driven mad
Between the protocols of tears and rapture.
Locked in our fated and contiguous selves,
These worlds that too much agitate each other,
Interdependencies from hip to head,
Twin principalities both slave and free,
We coexist, proclaiming Peace together.
Tell me no lies! We are divided nations
With malcontents by thousands in our streets,
These thousands torn by inbred revolutions.
A triumph is demanded, not moral victories
Deduced from small advances, small retreats.
Are the gods of our fathers not still daemonic?
On the steps of the Capitol
The outraged lion of our years roars panic,
And we suffer the guilty cowardice of the will,
Gathering its bankrupt slogans up for flight
Like gold from ruined treasuries.
And yet, and yet, although the murmur rises,
We are what we are, and only life surprises.

                                        Stanley Kunitz

THE SONG OF THE DEAD SOLDIER

For seven years at school I named
 Our kings, their wars—if these were won—
A boy trained simple as we come,
 I read of an island in the sun,
 Where the Queen of Love was born.

At seventeen the postman brought,
 Into the room—my place of birth—
Some correspondence from the Crown,
 Demanding that with guns I earn,
 The modern shilling I was worth.

Lucky for me that I could read,
 Lucky for me our captain said,
You'll see the world for free my son,
 You're posted to an island John,
 Where the Queen of Love was born.

So twenty weeks went by and by,
 My back was straightened out my eye
Dead true as any button shone,
 And nine white-bellied porpoise led
 Our ship of shillings through the sun.

We landed with our drums and clad
 In war suits worth ten well-taxed pounds—
The costliest I ever had—
 Our foreign shoulders crossed the town,
 The Queen of Love our coloured flag.

And three by three through our curfew,
 Mother we marched like black and tan,
Singing to match our captain's cheers,
 Then I drank my eyes out of my head
 And wet Her shilling with my fears.

When morning came our captain bold
 Said the island shaped like an ass' skin
Must be kept calm, must be patrolled,
 For outposts are the heart and soul
 Of empire, love, and lawful rule.

I did not know to serve meant kill,
    And I did not see the captain fall,
As my life went out through a bullet hole,
    Mother, I said, your womb is done,
    Did they spend your English shilling well?

And then I saw a hag whose eyes
    Were big as medals and grey as lead,
I called my rifle but it was dead,
    Our captain roared but my ears went dud,
    The hag kissed warm, we met in blood.

English shilling—Queen of Love.

Christopher Logue

WHAT WERE THEY LIKE?

(1) Did the people of Viet Nam
    use lanterns of stone?
(2) Did they hold ceremonies
    to reverence the opening of buds?
(3) Were they inclined to quiet laughter?
(4) Did they use bone and ivory,
    jade and silver, for ornament?
(5) Had they an epic poem?
(6) Did they distinguish between speech and singing?

(1) Sir, their light hearts turned to stone.
    It is not remembered whether in gardens
    stone lanterns illumined pleasant ways.
(2) Perhaps they gathered once to delight in blossom,
    but after the children were killed
    there were no more buds.
(3) Sir, laughter is bitter to the burned mouth.
(4) A dream ago, perhaps. Ornament is for joy.
    All the bones were charred.
(5) It is not remembered. Remember,
    most were peasants; their life
    was in rice and bamboo.
    When peaceful clouds were reflected in the paddies
    and the water buffalo stepped surely along terraces,
    maybe fathers told their sons old tales.

119

When bombs smashed those mirrors
there was time only to scream.
(6) There is an echo yet
of their speech which was like a song.
It was reported their singing resembled
the flight of moths in moonlight.
Who can say? It is silent now.

Denise Levertov

DEFENCE

She arrived late, with this motto:
'Time used in reconnaissance
Is not time lost.' Useful hint
On how efficient our defences
Would be. Sent from the Home Office
On 'Work of some importance'.
And 'The first thing' she said
'Is that there will be four minutes
Of preparation before
The thing is dropped. You should
Instruct persons to stand
In the centre of what room
They like—for the blast,
Unlike the bombs of the previous war,
Will draw the walls out.
There will be no crushing
Of flesh. Instead
On all sides walls will reveal
The citizen unharmed.' Here a question,
But 'No' she said 'we have
From our *Intelligence*
Absolute assurance
Our capital is not targeted.'
Total warfare, by arrangement.
And she was sure, when pressed.
'But there will be devastation,
As we now suspect, in radius
Of forty-four miles.
The water will be infected;
The light from the thing, astonishing;
Which though surprised by, we should

Not look at; but shelter
Behind some object "to reduce
Damage to the tissue"
From radiation; or shelter
Under brown paper;
Or, if you can,—
Sheets soaked in urine.'

So women who crochet, stop that;
Men labouring whose issue is
The two-handed house, set that aside.
Girls big and delicate
With child, turn on your side;
You will melt. The ravelling spider
And the scorpion whose prongs itch
Will fuse in a viscoid
Tar, black as a huge fly.
The whole of nature
Is preying upon.
Let man, whose mind is large,
Legislate for
All passionate things,
All sensate things: the sensuous
Grass, whose speech is all
In its sharp, bending blade.
Leave not a leaf, a stone
That rested on the dead
To its own dissolution.

She left then,
As if she were with her feet
Turning an enormous,
If man-made, pearl
As means of locomotion.

Jon Silkin

THE HORSES

Barely a twelvemonth after
The seven days war that put the world to sleep,
Late in the evening the strange horses came.
By then we had made our covenant with silence.

But in the first few days it was so still
We listened to our breathing and were afraid.
On the second day
The radios failed; we turned the knobs; no answer.
On the third day a warship passed us, heading north,
Dead bodies piled on the deck. On the sixth day
A plane plunged over us into the sea. Thereafter
Nothing. The radios dumb;
And still they stand in corners of our kitchens,
And stand, perhaps, turned on, in a million rooms
All over the world. But now if they should speak,
If on a sudden they should speak again,
If on the stroke of noon a voice should speak,
We would not listen, we would not let it bring
That bad old world that swallowed its children quick
At one great gulp. We would not have it again.
Sometimes we think of the nations lying asleep,
Curled blindly in impenetrable sorrow,
And then the thought confounds us with its strangeness.

The tractors lie about our fields; at evening
They look like dank sea-monsters couched and waiting.
We leave them where they are and let them rust:
'They'll moulder away and be like other loam.'
We make our oxen drag our rusty ploughs,
Long laid aside. We have gone back
Far past our fathers' land.
                              And then, that evening
Late in the summer the strange horses came.
We heard a distant tapping on the road,
A deepening drumming; it stopped, went on again
And at the corner changed to hollow thunder.
We saw the heads
Like a wild wave charging and were afraid.
We had sold our horses in our fathers' time
To buy new tractors. Now they were strange to us
As fabulous steeds set on an ancient shield
Or illustrations in a book of knights.
We did not dare go near them. Yet they waited,
Stubborn and shy, as if they had been sent
By an old command to find our whereabouts
And that long-lost archaic companionship.
In the first moment we had never a thought
That they were creatures to be owned and used.

Among them were some half-a-dozen colts
Dropped in some wilderness of the broken world,
Yet new as if they had come from their own Eden.
Since then they have pulled our ploughs and borne our loads,
But that free servitude still can pierce our hearts.
Our life is changed; their coming our beginning.

Edwin Muir

Notes

THE RUNAWAY (p.1)

1.3   *Morgan*: an American breed of light horse. Originally all these horses were descended from a stallion owned by Justin Morgan about 1800.

1.20   *bin*: a receptacle for holding corn.

A MARCH CALF (p.1)

1.2   *quiffed*: with curly hair looking as though it is plastered down on his forehead.

1.19   *syllogism*: a syllogism is a form of reasoning that deals with one comparatively small, isolated piece of logic, rather than a general philosophy of life. The calf thinks only of his own small part of life, just as the creator of a syllogism is taking a limited view.

AN OTTER (p.3)

Hughes contrasts the otter living naturally (ll. 1-20) with the otter hiding under water from the hunt (ll. 21-31). He also contrasts the live otter (ll. 1-38) with the dead otter (ll. 39-40). A vermin-pole (1.7) was the gibbet on which a gamekeeper hung the animals that he had shot or trapped, because he classed them as vermin.

THE JAGUAR (p.9)

The coiled-up boa-constrictor seems a dead fossil compared with this vibrant, unconquered jaguar. The comparison with a fossil suggests both the dull colour and the inertness of the boa-constrictor.

The jaguar's eyes (ll. 12-13) pierce the darkness of his cage and the crowd of spectators outside, as though they were electric drills. They are about to explode, like a short train of gunpowder that forms a fuse which will create an explosion almost immediately (1.13). Moreover, the jaguar's defiant, active stride has created a kind of freedom (1.18).

Ted Hughes wrote this poem when he worked as a dishwasher at London Zoo and could see the caged jaguar from his sink.

HAWK ROOSTING (p.11)

It must be emphasised that Hughes is thinking of a genuine hawk and is not using the hawk as a symbol of a selfishly successful type of human.

HOMAGE TO A GOVERNMENT (p.17)

The statues are to explorers and soldiers who added territories to the British Empire in past centuries, and in many cases brought these countries peace and progress.

THE PERSIAN VERSION (p.18)

Today every government employs propagandists, some of whom are even more untruthful than others. In this poem Graves is satirising this unhappy trend in modern history. If the Persian government in 415 B.C. had had a propaganda ministry, this is how it would have disguised what really happened at Marathon—the Persians invaded Greece and suffered a major defeat.

TO OUR CATCHMENT BOARD (p.21)

1.14 *snags*: piece of rough timber embedded in the river bottom and so impeding navigation.

THIS LANDSCAPE, THESE PEOPLE (p.25)

In the first section, Ghose describes his feelings during the eight years that he has spent in England. He has come to England at the age of seventeen and is writing the poem when he is twenty-five.

In the second section he describes how he enjoyed life in India till he was seventeen; then he decided that there was no real freedom left in India—possibly because he is a Muslim.

In the third section he explains that at twenty-five he feels more at home in England than in India—presumably because it allows its citizens more freedom.

THE EXPLOSION (p.29)

When Larkin comes to the point in his story when there is an explosion in the coal mine, he breaks off his narrative and leaves us with one last picture—the miners' wives had telepathic visions of their husbands as they died.

FROM SCHOOL'S OUT (p.31)

A. S. Neill founded an independent school at Summerhill at which pupils had considerable freedom—e.g. they could decide whether to attend lessons or not. Ivan Illich was born in Austria, but lives in the USA. His book *Deschooling Society* (1971) argues that children would learn more if schools were abolished, and stresses how much children can learn from radio and cassettes in preference to schoolbooks.

1.3 *barbola*: embellishment of small articles by attaching to them coloured models of flowers and fruits.

1.15 *Stakhanovites*: Soviet workers who were rewarded by the state for increasing their output to an exceptional extent.

INEXPENSIVE PROGRESS (p.32)

Sir John Betjeman is sarcastic. He tells his readers (the general public) to do exactly what he hates to see us do, and hopes we will stop doing. For instance, we have allowed chain-stores to erect similar shops in the High Streets of all our towns. Consequently our towns look more alike—and more American—every year.

A CURSE (p.33)

Diesel (1859-1913) lived in France, England, Germany and Switzerland in turn. He invented the engine named after him and he hoped that it would help the poorer, less-developed countries because it operates on cheaper fuel than petrol; but Auden accuses his invention of increasing air pollution.

1.24 *smith*: to make, in the way that a blacksmith makes a horse's shoe.

1.36 *brougham*: a closed carriage originally pulled by one horse but later driven by electricity.

TRANSLATION (p.34)

Roy Fuller pretends to be a Roman poet writing about A.D. 400 and regretting the decline of Roman civilisation. Fuller gloomily suggests that our present civilisation has similarily begun to decline. The *twelve-tone scale* (1.2) uses the twelve chromatic notes of the octave, arranged in a chosen order, without using a conventional key. In referring to it, Fuller is using a deliberate anachronism. His Roman poet speaks about new music in the way that Fuller's old-fashioned friends speak about some twentieth-century composers—notably Schoenberg. For instance, Constant Lambert in *Music Ho!* describes the music that uses the twelve-tone scale as 'the most abnormal movement music has ever known'.

EXECUTIVE (p.36)
Betjeman is portraying a man of whom he disapproves.

THE CLOTHES PIT (p.38)
These young women do not carry a copy of a fashionable paper in order to impress other people. They live in Terry Street, an unfashionable street in Hull.

ON THE MOVE (p.39)
Gunn is illustrating various examples of the instinct that impels some animals, some birds, and some humans to be always on the move. There are extreme examples which Gunn does not quote: for instance, salmon move from the distant parts of the Atlantic to spawn in British rivers. Gunn suggests that the jay moving about in the bushes, or the flock of birds moving larger distances, are obeying this instinct. So are the young men who ride their motorcycles long distances without an apparent purpose.

The poem's central characters, the roving motorcyclists, are derived from the film *The Wild Ones* in which Marlon Brando starred. The motorcyclists are young rebels who defy the authority of the old, but they are also obeying some fundamental human instinct. The last lines of the poem defend philosophically these motorcyclists who feel they must obey the instinct to keep moving.

THE RETIRED COLONEL (p.45)
Like the last wolf to survive in England and the last sturgeon to swim in the Thames (before it became polluted) the retired Colonel is the last of his kind. He looks as though he was one of the British Army who endured a long siege at Mafeking (1899-1900) in the South African War.

THE UNKNOWN CITIZEN (p.46)
W. H. Auden wrote this ironical poem after he had emigrated to the USA. He deliberately sets out to use many American words and details, though the name 'The Unknown Soldier' (which its title parodies) is common to many countries.

THE SOLITUDE OF MR POWERS (p.53)
Cavalleria Rusticana and *Il Pagliacci* are two short operas which usually make up a double bill.

A PRAYER FOR MY DAUGHTER (p.56)
In 1916 the Southern Irish rose in rebellion against the English; and in 1922, after several years of bitter civil war, Southern Ireland obtained its independence. W. B. Yeats, although a Protestant, sympathised with the

rebels who fought to create the new state. Yet he felt that too many of the beautiful Irish women who were his friends (notably Maud Gonne) had become extremists in the Irish cause, and had sacrificed too much—their own humanity and femininity.

In 1917 Yeats married, when fifty-two years old. He went to live in western Ireland: writing in 1919 he expresses the hope that his very young daughter will not be too beautiful—because very beautiful women, such as the mythical Helen of Troy and the real Maud Gonne, had caused so much tragedy. Like many fathers today, he hopes that his daughter will not grow up to be an extremist.

Yeats refers to two very beautiful women in Greek mythology who chose the wrong man and caused much unhappiness to themselves and others. Helen of Troy was bored by life in Greece with her husband, Menelaus, but suffered much from the actions of her foolish lover, Paris. Venus, who was born out of the foam of the sea, chose as her husband the lame blacksmith of the Gods, Vulcan, and grew tired of him.

TARKINGTON, THOU SHOULDST BE LIVING IN THIS HOUR (p.58)
The title is a humorous reference to a sonnet by Wordsworth which begins:
    'Milton, thou shouldst be living at this hour.'
Tarkington (Booth) was an American novelist who paid more attention to analysis of character than to his stories. Presumably he would find the characters of Ogden Nash's adolescents interesting to analyse.

O THE VALLEY IN THE SUMMER (p.66)
The whole poem has an irresistible rhythm, and one which prevents us from ever taking the poem seriously. We are amused at the ridiculous hyperboles of the love-sick, forsaken woman, which sound like a parody of the words of popular songs. There is an amusing contrast between the extravagance of the woman's language and the inscrutable brutality of the man's behaviour; the poem is thus an amusing exaggeration of some of the aspects of pop songs about love.

A SUBALTERN'S LOVE-SONG (p.68)
1.13 *euonymus*: a spindle-tree.

WEDDING-WIND (p.69)
The imaginary speaker is a young bride who married a farmer on the previous day; they have spent their honeymoon night on his farm. In the night her husband had to get up to close a stable door that the wind had blown open. Now next day it is still windy, and the wind blows the washing on the clothes-line to and fro. She feels that the wind is a symbol of her own vitality and happiness.

In ll. 17-20 her joy strings her actions and feelings together just as a thread holds beads in place. She is so happy and excited that she wonders whether she will ever subside into an ordinary life as unexcited as *sleep*.

In ll. 20-23 her husband and herself, enjoying limitless happiness, are compared to cattle drinking from lakes that will never dry up.

THE GAME (p.75)

As Abse watches Cardiff City he thinks of great players who played for them in the past, such as Keenor, and also great players who played for other clubs, such as Dixie Dean (Everton). Because Abse, like most supporters of the home side, regards the other side as devils, he applies to them words such as *Lucifer* and *infernal*.

SPRING OFFENSIVE (p.103)

In *Spring Offensive* Owen contrasts the natural beauty of the countryside through which the soldiers first advanced with the unnatural hail of fire that met them as soon as they attacked. One of Owen's problems was how to make use of his talent for romantic description; here he uses it relevantly as a necessary element in his contrast. The phrase *some say* in 1.37 illustrates that Owen cannot decide whether to go on believing in Christianity.

DULCE ET DECORUM EST (p.104)

Owen brands as a lie the view of the Roman poet, Horace, that 'It is sweet and proper to die for the fatherland.'

Five-Nines (1.8) are 5.9-in. shells, which were dropping poison gas.

THE SENTRY (p.105)

The last line must mean that the casualty has become either blind or mad. He claims to see a light that does not exist.

STRANGE MEETING (p.106)

In the early lines Owen uses a new type of assonance to suggest that noises of battle penetrate the tunnel of his dreams: e.g. *titanic* echoes *granite*. In this poem, as in some (but not all) of his poems, Owens uses a para-rhyme, e.g. he rhymes *cot* with *cat* and not with *pot*. Though various French and Welsh poets had used this type of rhyme before, Owen probably reinvented it himself.

In this poem a dead German is speaking (ll. 26-30), and he gives an ironically true forecast of the future of Germany after 1918. He regrets that the deaths of men like himself have destroyed their chances to make a better world. Owen foresees that the First World War will change the direction of history for the worse.

ULTIMA RATIO REGUM (p.109)

This poem describes a young man killed in the Spanish Civil War (1936-39). In this war Franco led a right-wing revolt against the left-wing government. Hitler and Mussolini helped Franco, hoping to use Spanish bases in the Second World War which they were preparing for. In Britain and France members of the right-wing tended to sympathise with Franco; liberals, socialists and communists tended to sympathise with the Spanish government.

from AUTUMN JOURNAL (p.110)

In 1938 Hitler threatened to invade Czechoslovakia. Neville Chamberlain, the British Prime Minister, knew that Britain lacked the up-to-date aircraft, anti-aircraft guns and tanks to win a war. But he overestimated Germany's preparedness. After two months of propaganda speeches by Hitler and after two meetings between him and Chamberlain, at the end of September 1938 Chamberlain agreed to give Hitler part of Czechoslovakia and Hitler promised to keep the peace. In 1939 Hitler broke these promises; he seized the rest of Czechoslovakia, and invaded Poland. By then both Britain and Germany were better prepared for war than they had been in 1938. In *Autumn Journal* (a diary in verse) MacNeice describes the feelings of the British public during August and September 1938 as they waited to see whether war would come, and as they watched anti-aircraft batteries being sited in London.

UNSEEN FIRE (p.111)
Currey stresses how bomber pilots and anti-aircraft gunners both belonged to highly technical branches of warfare; they carried on destruction impersonally at a distance. R. N. Currey was serving with an anti-aircraft battery.

THE EVACUEE (p.112)
A young girl living in a town likely to be bombed—where she would hear the siren, i.e. the air-raid warning (1.5)—has been evacuated to a farm in the more peaceful countryside.

WATCHING POST (p.113)
C. Day Lewis was serving in the Home Guard.

NAMING OF PARTS (p.114)
This poem illustrates the more boring side of training to fight (after the Second World War had begun). In each stanza a dull sergeant gives part of his lecture, then the listener's mind begins to wander.

VERGISSMEINNICHT (p.115)
Douglas fought against the German army in North Africa.

FOREIGN AFFAIRS (p.116)
One of the unexpected and grim features of life since 1945 has been the spread of small wars in many continents. Often one state has sent guerilla troops to fight another without declaring war.

THE SONG OF THE DEAD SOLDIER (p.118)
The dead soldier has gone to Cyprus, where, in the early 1950s, most of the Greek inhabitants carried on a guerilla war against the British until Cyprus was granted independence. This independence has been complicated by wars between the Greek and Turkish communities in Cyprus and by the fact that the British have kept some bases in Cyprus.

WHAT WERE THEY LIKE? (p.119)
From 1966 to 1975 the Americans tried, in vain, to prevent the communist Vietnamese from taking control of their country and from overthrowing the corrupt right-wing government of Vietnam. Denise Levertov accuses the Americans of killing Vietnamese civilians in a war that they could never win.

DEFENCE (p.120)
This poem implies the question—what would a Third World War be like?

THE HORSES (p.121)
Muir imagines that some people survive a Third World War in a remote place such as northern Scotland.

Index of Authors

131

Acknowledgements

Thanks are due to the authors (or their executors), their representatives and publishers mentioned in the following list for their kind permission to reproduce copyright material:

Dannie Abse: 'The Death of Aunt Alice' and 'Driving Home' from *Car Journeys*, and 'The Game' from *Collected Poems 1948-1976* (Hutchinson Ltd).

John Arlott: 'Cricket at Swansea', 'Cricket at Worcester 1938'.

W. H. Auden: 'A Curse', 'Embassy', 'O the Valley in the Summer' and 'The Unknown Citizen' from *Collected Poems* ed. Mendelson (Faber and Faber Ltd).

Julian Bell: 'Woods and Kestrels'.

Anne Beresford: 'The Romanies in Town' from *The Lair* (Rapp and Whiting Ltd).

John Betjeman: 'Executive' from *A Nip in the Air;* 'Cornish Cliffs' and 'Inexpensive Progress' from *High and Low;* 'Hunter Trials' and 'Seaside Golf' from *A Few Late Chrysanthemums;* and 'A Subaltern's Love Song' from *New Bats in Old Belfries* (John Murray (Publishers) Ltd).

Edmund Blunden: 'To Our Catchment Board'. By permission of A. D. Peters & Co. Ltd.

Alan Bold: 'My First Sweetheart'.

Alan Brownjohn: 'Office Party' from *The Lion's Mouth* (Macmillan Ltd, London and Basingstoke).

Allan Burgis: 'The Great War on TV' from *Moving Pictures* (Platform Poets).

Norman Cameron: 'Public-House Confidence' from *The Collected Poems of Norman Cameron* (The Hogarth Press Ltd). By permission of the Literary Executor.

John Cassidy: 'Leopard' and 'The Bulb Field'.

Richard Church: 'Housing Scheme' from *Collected Poems* (Heinemann Ltd). By permission of the Executor of the Estate of Richard Church.

Stuart Conn: 'To my Father' from *An Ear to the Ground* (Hutchinson Ltd).

Tony Connor: 'Entering the City' and 'Lovers in Clowes Park' from *Lodgers;* and 'Old Men' from *In the Happy Valley* (Oxford University Press).

Stanley Cook: 'Pigeon Cotes in Penistone Road, Sheffield'.

R. N. Currey: 'Unseen Fire' from *This Other Planet* (Routledge & Kegan Paul Ltd).

C. Day Lewis: 'Sheepdog Trials in Hyde Park' from *The Gate* (Jonathan Cape Ltd); and 'Watching Post' from *Collected Poems 1954* (Jonathan Cape Ltd and The Hogarth Press Ltd). By permission of the Executors of the Estate of C. Day Lewis.

Paul Dehn: 'Gutter Press' from *The Fern on the Rock* (Hamish Hamilton Ltd). Copyright © Dehn Enterprises 1965, 1976.

Keith Douglas: 'Vergissmeinnicht' from *The Complete Poems of Keith Douglas* edited by Desmond Graham (Oxford University Press).

Douglas Dunn: 'The Clothes Pit' from *Terry Street* (Faber and Faber Ltd).

D. J. Enright: 'Monuments of Hiroshima' from *Bread Rather than Water* (Secker & Warburg Ltd).

Gavin Ewart: 'Sonnet: Mother Love'.

Robert Frost: 'The Runaway' from *The Poetry of Robert Frost* edited by Edward Connery Lathem (Jonathan Cape Ltd). By permission of the Executors of the Estate of Robert Frost and the editor.

Roy Fuller: 'Translation' from *Collected Poems* (Andre Deutsch Ltd).

Karen Gershon: 'Race' from *Selected Poems* (Gollancz Ltd).

Zulfikar Ghose: 'Geography Lesson', 'This Landscape, These People', 'Preservation of Landscapes' and 'Surf Rider'.

Robert Graves: 'Not at Home', 'The Persian Version', 'A Slice of Wedding Cake', and 'Symptoms of Love' from *Collected Poems* (Cassell and Co. Ltd).

Thom Gunn: 'Black Jackets' from *My Sad Captains;* and 'On the Move' from *Sense of Movement* (Faber and Faber Ltd).

Seamus Heaney: 'Twice Shy' from *Death of a Naturalist* (Faber and Faber Ltd).

John Heath-Stubbs: 'The Starling' from *The Blue-fly in his Head* (Oxford University Press).

Phoebe Hesketh: 'Blue Tits'.

Philip Hobsbaum: 'Provincial Undergraduate' from *The Place's Fault and Other Poems* (Macmillan Ltd).

David Holbrook: 'The Return' from *Against the Cruel Frost* (Putnam).

Ted Hughes: 'Hawk Roosting', 'An Otter' and 'The Retired Colonel' from *Lupercal;* 'Jaguar' from *The Hawk in the Rain;* and 'A March Calf' from *Season Songs* (Faber and Faber Ltd).

Elizabeth Jennings: 'Absence', 'The Climbers' and 'The Young Ones' from *Selected Poems* (Carcanet Press Ltd).

James Kirkup: 'A Visit to Brontëland' from *A Spring Journey.*

Stanley Kunitz: 'Foreign Affairs' from *The Terrible Threshold* (Secker & Warburg Ltd).

Philip Larkin: 'The Explosion' and 'Homage to a Government' from *High Windows;* 'Here' from *The Whitsun Wedding* (Faber and Faber Ltd); and 'Wedding-Wind' from *The Less Deceived* (The Marvell Press).

D. H. Lawrence: 'Kangaroo' from *The Complete Poems of D. H. Lawrence* (Heinemann Ltd). By permission of Laurence Pollinger Ltd and The Executors of the Estate of Mrs Frieda Lawrence Ravagli.

Denise Levertov: 'What Were They Like?' from *The Sorrow Dance* (New Directions Publishing Corporation).

Alun Lewis: 'Goodbye' from *Ha! Ha! Among the Trumpets* (George Allen & Unwin (Publishers) Ltd).

Maurice Lindsay: 'Farm Woman' from *Collected Poems* (Paul Harris Publishing, Edinburgh).

Christopher Logue: 'Song of the Dead Soldier'. Copyright © Christopher Logue 1959.

George Macbeth: 'Owl'.

Norman MacCaig: 'Edinburgh Courtyard in July' from *A Common Grace,* 'November Night, Edinburgh' from *The Sinai Sort,* 'Progress' from *Surroundings,* and 'Solitary Crow' from *Rings on a Tree* (The Hogarth Press Ltd).

Hugh MacDiarmid: 'The Two Parents' (Granada Publishing Ltd).

Louis MacNeice: '*from* Autumn Journal' and 'Indoor Sports' from *The Collected Poems of Louis MacNeice* (Faber and Faber Ltd).

Edwin Morgan: 'Hyena' from *Glasgow to Saturn* and 'School's Out' from *The New Divan* (Carcanet Press Ltd); 'An Addition to the Family: for M.L.', 'Good Friday' and 'Strawberries' from *The Second Life* (Edinburgh University Press).

Edwin Muir: 'The Horses' from *The Collected Poems of Edwin Muir* (Faber and Faber Ltd).

Ogden Nash: 'The Solitude of Mr Powers' and 'Tarkington' from *Collected Verse* (J. M. Dent & Sons Ltd). By permission of the Executors of the Estate of Ogden Nash.

Norman Nicholson: 'On the Closing of Millom Ironworks' from *A Local Habitation* and 'South Cumberland, 10 May 1945' from *Five Rivers* (Faber and Faber Ltd); 'Millom Cricket Field'.

Leslie Norris: 'A Small War' from *Mountains, Polecats, Pheasants and Other Elegies* (Chatto and Windus Ltd).

Wilfred Owen: '*Dulce et Decorum Est*', 'The Sentry', 'Spring Offensive' and 'Strange Meeting' from *The Collected Poems of Wilfred Owen* edited by C. Day Lewis (Chatto and Windus Ltd).

Eden Philpotts: 'Houses'.

Ezra Pound: 'The River-Merchant's Wife' from *Collected Shorter Poems* (Faber and Faber Ltd).

John Pudney: 'Aunts Watching Television' from *Sixpenny Songs* (The Bodley Head).

Theobald Purcell-Buret: 'The Diver'.

Herbert Read: 'Night Ride' from *Collected Poems* (Macmillan).

Henry Reed: 'Naming of Parts' from *A Map of Verona* (Jonathan Cape Ltd).

Siegfried Sassoon: 'Memorial Tablet'. By permission of the Executor of the Estate of Siegfried Sassoon.

Vernon Scannell: 'A Mystery at Euston'.

Ian Serraillier: 'The Summit' from *Everest Climbed* in *The Windmill Book of Ballads* (Heinemann Educational Books Ltd). © Ian Serraillier 1955.

Jon Silkin: 'The Cunning of an Age' and 'Defence'.

James Simmons: 'Leeds 2'.

Wole Soyinka: 'Telephone Conversation'.

Stephen Spender: '*Ultima Ratio Regum*' from *Collected Poems* (Faber and Faber Ltd).

Edward Storey: 'In Memory of My Grandfather' from *North Bank Night* (Chatto and Windus Ltd).

A.S.J. Tessimond: 'Attack on the Ad-man'. By permission of the Literary Executor, Hubert Nicholson.

R.S. Thomas: 'The Evacuee' and 'The View from the Window' from *Selected Poems* (Granada Publishing Ltd).

Andrew Waterman: 'Mother' from *Livings* (The Marvell Press).

Vernon Watkins: 'The Heron'. By permission of G.M. Watkins.

Herbert Williams: 'Jones the Grocer'.

William Carlos Williams: 'A Negro Woman' and 'This is Just to Say' from *Pictures from Brueghel and Other Poems* (New Directions Publishing Corporation, New York). Copyright © William Carlos Williams 1955.

David Wright: 'Swift'. By permission of A.D. Peters & Co. Ltd.

W.B. Yeats: 'A Prayer for my Daughter' from *Collected Poems* (Macmillan Ltd, London). By permission of M.B. Yeats and Miss Anne Yeats.

Andrew Young: 'Wiltshire Downs' from *Complete Poems* (Secker & Warburg Ltd).